To will —

Best wishes,
Barry Johnston

Also by Barry Johnston

Round Mr Horne: The Life of Kenneth Horne
Johnners: The Life of Brian

and as editor

An Evening With Johnners
Letters Home 1926–1945
A Delicious Slice of Johnners
Another Slice of Johnners
A Further Slice of Johnners
The Wit of Golf

THE WIT
OF CRICKET

Compiled by Barry Johnston

Illustrated by John Ireland

HODDER

First published in Great Britain in 2009 by Hodder & Stoughton
An Hachette UK company

First published in paperback in 2010

6

A CIP catalogue record for this title is available from the British Library.

ISBN 978 0 340 97889 4

Typeset in MT Sabon by Hewer Text UK Ltd, Edinburgh

Printed and bound in the UK by CPI Group (UK) Ltd, Croydon, CR0 4YY

Hodder & Stoughton policy is to use papers that are natural,
renewable and recyclable products and made from wood grown in
sustainable forests. The logging and manufacturing processes are expected
to conform to the environmental regulations of the country of origin.

Hodder & Stoughton Ltd
338 Euston Road
London NW1 3BH

www.hodder.co.uk

To Blowers, Dickie, Sir Frederick,
Johnners and Richie
and Bearders

CONTENTS

FOREWORD

I grew up listening to my father, Brian Johnston, telling jokes and stories. He remembered funny anecdotes in the same way that other people collect stamps, and he loved retelling them in his after-dinner speeches and in his one-man show *An Evening with Johnners*.

Most of those stories were about cricket – it is a game that has inspired more humour than any other sport. The popularity of my father's recording of *An Evening with Johnners* led me to produce two CDs of *The Wit of Cricket* which have both been a huge – and surprising – commercial success. So I began compiling this anthology from the abundant harvest provided by five of the greatest raconteurs the game has ever known – Brian Johnston, Dickie Bird, Henry Blofeld, Richie Benaud and Fred Trueman. Then I looked for other cricket stories from home and abroad which would add spice to this already potent brew and discovered a curious phenomenon.

Cricket stories can be rather like Chinese whispers. Every time an anecdote is retold a small detail gets altered or exaggerated so that after a while it bears little relation to what actually happened. The rise of the internet has made things even more complicated, with cricket fans being able to post their own versions of stories on websites and in chatrooms. In researching this book I have read accounts of well-known incidents where the year, the ground and most of the players mentioned were all wrong. An anecdote involving Viv Richards in the 1970s turns up in the 1990s as being about Sachin Tendulkar or Ricky Ponting.

Sometimes it doesn't really matter, as long as it makes you laugh, but wherever possible in this book I have tried to include the original version. I have gathered together anecdotes from past and present Test and county players, as well as the most famous cricketing sledges, plus the gaffes and giggles in the *Test Match Special* commentary box. The wonderful thing about cricket literature is that it continues to thrive, so I have also been able to include amusing stories from *Penguins Stopped Play*, *Batting on the Bosphorus*, *Rain Men* and *Fatty Batter*, books that have become modern cricket classics.

Cricket is often said to be a funny game. Now you can read why. Here is my choice of the funniest jokes, the most humorous anecdotes and the wittiest stories as told by former and current Test players, club cricketers, umpires, commentators and journalists.

I hope you enjoy reading them as much as I have enjoyed compiling them.

Barry Johnston
2009

CAPTAINS

Barry Johnston:

In October 1998, during the Second Test against Pakistan at Peshawar, the Australian captain Mark 'Tubby' Taylor tied Sir Donald Bradman's sixty-eight-year-old Australian Test record of 334 runs. Although the team voted for him to continue to bat the following morning, Taylor declared his side's innings closed after he had tied the record. The Don, who was then ninety years old, sent Taylor a telegram of congratulations.

Shortly afterwards in Australia a newspaper advertisement for toilet paper appeared. It read: 'Tubby, it's good to see you with the runs again!'

Dickie Bird:

A former Hampshire captain is Nick Pocock, who once played in a benefit match for Ken Barrington in Amsterdam, on a very hot day. He got quite a few runs, and when he came off the field, sweat was pouring out of him. His shirt was wet through. He wasn't too sure where the showers were, never having played on the ground before, but Surrey's Ron Tindall was quick to help.

'We've made arrangements,' said Ron, 'to shower in that house on the other side of the road. If you don't fancy a shower, you can have a bath.'

So Nick made his way over, undressed, helped himself to a whisky and settled down to soak in the bath. He had been luxuriating in the tub for a few minutes when, to his amazement, a woman walked in. Nick didn't know how to cover his embarrassment, and she was just as shocked as he was. 'What on earth do you think you are doing in my bath?' she demanded.

Nick stuttered, 'I'm playing in the cricket match across the road and we've been given permission to shower and bath here.'

The woman shouted for her husband, who stormed in red-faced. 'Who are you? I've given no one permission to shower, bath, drink my whisky or anything else. Now clear off before I call the police.'

When Nick returned to the pavilion, Tindall popped his head round the door and asked, 'Enjoy your shower, Nick?'

Brian Johnston:

There's a different sort of captain I rather like – Keith Miller, the jovial chap from Australia. A marvellous figure of a man. He loved hitting sixes, bowling bouncers and backing horses. He loved women and they loved him. He didn't worry much about tactics or laws, but he just enjoyed playing with his friends on, and off, the field.

There's a lovely story about him. He didn't captain Australia, but he captained New South Wales and he was leading them out once, walking twenty yards in front, a majestic figure, tossing his hair.

A chap called Jimmy Burke ran up and tugged his sweater and said, 'Nugget!' (He used to call him 'Nugget'.) 'Nugget, Nugget, we've got twelve men on the field!'

Miller didn't pause. He went walking on and said, 'Well, tell one of them to bugger off then!'

Graeme Fowler:

In my first season of opening regularly for Lancashire, I was batting with Clive Lloyd, when he called me down to him mid-over. It was getting to a stage where we needed to accelerate, and he was captain at the time, so I went down the wicket and asked, 'What?'

He looked down at me and said, 'My piles are killing me!' And he turned round and walked back.

I said to him afterwards, 'What on earth did you do that for?'

He said, 'Well, I thought you were looking a bit tense!'

Dickie Bird:

Keith Miller was one of the great Australian characters before and after the war. He was a bit forgetful at times, and one day the team was all set to take the field when Keith was asked, 'Where's old so-and-so?'

'No idea,' said Keith. 'Is he supposed to be playing?'

'Yes,' came the reply, '. . . and you were supposed to be giving him a lift!'

Simon Hughes:

In a knock-out match against Surrey at The Oval, the galumphing Sylvester Clarke produced a terrifying spell with the new ball, bulldozing through Middlesex's top order. The Middlesex captain Mike Brearley began the procession, getting out in the first over caught behind off a flier. His simmering mood was inflamed by Ted, the old Cockney attendant in the pavilion, saying innocently, ''Ere, Mike, wot you doin' back so early? Ain't they started yet?'

Brearley nearly wrapped the bat around him.

Henry Blofeld:

Colin Ingleby-Mackenzie was the flamboyant captain of Hampshire who led them to their first county championship in 1961. Hampshire's training diet in those days used to be 'wine, women and song'. Colin was once asked what time he liked his players to be in bed and he said, 'By nine.' When someone said, 'Isn't that a bit early?' he replied, 'Well, play does start at eleven thirty!'

Dickie Bird:

New Zealand have never been one of the strongest cricketing nations, but they have always retained an ability to laugh at themselves. With his team in desperate straits on one tour of England, captain Ken Rutherford gave a perfect example of how a little bit of light-hearted repartee can deflect criticism, and lift the mood at a time of crisis.

He was asked by a journalist if he found it personally distressing to be captain of the New Zealand ship. Rutherford looked at the journalist, smiled, cupped a hand to his ear and said, 'Sorry, I didn't quite catch that. Did you say *ship*?'

Chris England: Balham to Bollywood

At my level, being a good captain is at least as much about having the ability to cajole people into giving up half a Sunday as it is about motivation, skill or tactics. This means that I often find myself pitted against the type of captain I fear becoming above all others – the passenger captain. He is alarmingly common in the cricketing circles in which I move, and his approach has too many similarities to my own for me to sleep easy at nights.

He is the captain who organises a team, and puts himself through all the torture that entails, because he knows he wouldn't ever get a game otherwise. Typically, he will begin his career by forging a side from a bunch of old college mates or work colleagues, fixing up the odd friendly here and there. Soon he will move on to building up a fixture list of more frightening proportions, until the team threatens to take over the entire summer.

He makes all the telephone calls, he makes all the teas. He frets all week about some dilettante who doesn't let him know whether he can actually play until the morning of the match. When the dilettante does finally withdraw, usually because otherwise he'll only see his girlfriend for six days in the week, the passenger captain knocks himself out ringing everyone he knows trying to get an eleventh man. He turns up at the pub at lunchtime, twitching and sweating, having just persuaded someone who lived across the corridor from him at university fifteen years ago and whom he hasn't seen since to turn out for his team.

He then spends a will-sapping three-quarters of an hour trying to hurry his team out of the pub to actually start the game. He goes out to do the toss with the opposing captain, which he loses, and then scuttles off to pad up, because nobody else wants to open the batting. Instead of having a couple of balls lobbed at him to get his eye in, he trots around trying to get someone to do the scoring, begging others to put down the Sunday paper and do a couple of overs' umpiring.

Some years ago we played against an archetypal passenger captain. It happened that the team I had managed to put together for the occasion had only one decent bowler, and he hadn't appeared by the time the match got under way. As it turned out, he had left my painstakingly detailed directions to the ground by the phone and then gone to another completely different ground on the other side of London that he once vaguely remembered playing on. I thus was forced to open the bowling with someone who hadn't bowled in years, and wasn't really sure he could remember how to do it.

The umpires came out, followed by their openers. One, relaxed, swinging his arms, grinning, made his way to the non-striker's end with his pal the umpire. The other, the passenger captain, was wound tight as a coiled spring. His kit gleamed whiter than white. Brand-new pads and gloves, an expensive, new, freshly linseeded and as yet unmarked bat, and, amazingly, given my bowling attack, a bright spanking white helmet with a grille.

Grub, my makeshift opening bowler, shuffled in to begin the innings. As he brought his arm over, the ball slipped from his grasp a split second too soon and looped gently twenty feet up into the sky. As it arced slowly down the pitch some giggling broke out in the field, but nothing disturbed the awesomely tense concentration of the passenger captain. He kept his eye on the ball all the way, brand-new bat paused at the top of his backlift, just telling himself to wait, wait, wait and see if he would need to play the ball.

At the last instant, he seemed to realise that if he continued to keep his eye on the ball, the ball was actually going to smack him right in the eye. Perhaps not trusting his new grille, he ducked. The ball dropped over and behind his crouching form and, descending almost vertically now, landed perfectly on the top of middle stump, dislodging a single apologetic bail.

As I watched the passenger captain trudge disconsolately back to the pavilion to spend the rest of the innings either scoring or umpiring while his team-mates read the paper, what could I think, except: 'There but for the grace of God . . .'

Dickie Bird:

There can hardly have been a more endearing character at Essex than Brian 'Tonker' Taylor. They called him that because he loved to give the ball an almighty tonk. He was both captain and wicket-keeper, and under him Essex were never short of ideas for getting batsmen out. Like one time, when Tonker set out to trick a compulsive hooker into playing the shot that would most likely prove his undoing.

Sure enough, the batsman, unable to resist the temptation, hooked the ball high and hard and was brilliantly caught just inside the ropes. Tonker and his team were ecstatic – until they realised that the umpire had called 'no-ball'.

All eyes turned accusingly towards the bowler and his frustrated colleagues tore him off a right strip until the umpire explained that he had not called the bowler for over-stepping. He turned to Tonker. 'It was your fault, skipper,' he said to him. 'You've three men behind square-leg.' The laws allowed for only two.

Tonker looked round in disbelief. He counted once. He counted twice. And he counted again. Then the penny dropped. 'Don't tell me you were counting that chap right on the boundary edge,' he muttered menacingly.

'Of course,' replied the umpire.

Tonker exploded, 'That's not a fielder, you fool, that's the bloody ice-cream man!'

Ian Brayshaw:

Some suggest it is a mistake to appoint a bowler to captain a cricket team because he either bowls himself too little or too much. Legend has it that it was invariably a case of the latter when J.W.H.T. Douglas captained England. Bowlers in Douglas's teams were known to mutter to each other when a new batsman came in, 'You go on now and bowl him in, Mr Douglas . . . we'll come on later and bowl him out.'

One day Douglas had gone on for so long that one of them felt moved to approach him:

'Don't you think it's time we had a change in the attack, Mr Douglas?'

'You could be right,' came the reply. 'I'll have a go at the other end!'

Dickie Bird:

Brian Close was a great captain. He joined Somerset from Yorkshire in 1972 and provided the spark that was to ignite the county and turn them into a trophy-winning side. He proved inspirational with his fearless batting and fielding. He instilled discipline into the side and injected a new determination to succeed. The only problem with Closey was that nothing was ever his fault.

Once, at Trent Bridge, he went out to bat in a bid to avert a Barry Stead hat-trick. The scoreboard read 42 for 3. As he came out he had a quick word with the outgoing batsman, Richard Cooper. There was a hush as Stead came in, with nine men huddled round the bat. Ever the one to take the bull by the horns, Close aimed an almighty swipe at the hat-trick ball.

It was bold, brave and not as daft as it looked, because there was only one man, Nirmal Nannan, in the outfield. Unluckily for Close, although he made good contact, the ball seemed to be attracted like a magnet to Nannan's hands and the fielder took the catch. The ground erupted.

All was quiet, however, in the Somerset dressing room as the players waited for the inevitable explosion when Closey stormed in. Sure enough, he hurled his bat to the floor, glared at the unfortunate Cooper, and snarled, 'Bloody hell, lad, you said it were swingin', but you never said it were seamin' an' all!'

Barry Johnston:

By the start of October 2001, England captain Nasser Hussain's lack of success with the coin toss was becoming the stuff of legend. Back in February, long-suffering England cricket fans were already grumbling about the loss of eight tosses out of ten, the odds against which were about 22 to 1. By the end of the summer the England skipper had lost twelve tosses in a row, a stunning run with odds against of more than 4,000 to 1.

Then in October, on tour in Zimbabwe, Nasser Hussain was injured. Marcus Trescothick took over as England captain on 10 October for the fourth one-day international against Zimbabwe, in Bulawayo, and immediately won the toss. Three days later Hussain recovered and returned to the captaincy for the final match in the series – and promptly lost his thirteenth toss in a row!

Dickie Bird:

Robin Marlar was the captain of Sussex between 1955 and 1959 and it has been somewhat unfairly suggested that, while players followed David 'The Rev' Sheppard out of faith, and 'Lord Ted' Dexter out of loyalty, they followed Marlar out of sheer curiosity.

John Barclay became captain of the side in 1981. Barclay was an Old Etonian, as you can probably tell by his remark following a difficult decision he had to make when G.D. Mendis was batting for Sussex. Barclay declared with Mendis on 97 not out and chasing his fifth century in six innings. Said Barclay, 'Oh, I do hope he doesn't think I'm a swine and a cad!'

Martin Johnson:

There are many stories revolving around Brian Close's total belief in his own infallibility, the most quintessential of which was experienced by Peter Roebuck when Close was captain of Somerset. Roebuck, then right at the start of his career, was batting pretty well, unlike the veteran Close at the other end, who could barely lay bat on ball. At the end of an over Close wandered down the pitch for a chat, and Roebuck fondly imagined that he might just be in for a word of encouragement, if not praise.

'I don't know, lad,' sighed Close. 'Don't understand it. It's bloody unplayable at my end, but they're bowling complete rubbish to you!'

Dickie Bird:

Chris Tavaré was the captain of Somerset for three years between 1990 and 1993. There is no way, however, that Tavaré can be included among the list of big-hitting crowd-pleasers who have graced the Somerset county grounds through the years.

Journalist Martin Johnson once revealed that he used to carry a box of pigeons by way of insurance, just in case the telephone lines went down. One day, he said, it backfired on him. He was strapping an account of a six-hour Tavaré innings on to the pigeon's back when he realised that the poor bird had fallen into a deep coma. By the time he managed to revive it, the last edition of his paper had long gone!

John Barclay:

Middlesex v Sussex at Hove in 1980 – I toss up with Mike Brearley and win. Walking back to the pavilion to convey this news to the team, I was addressed by a lady at the boundary edge.

'Mr Barclay,' she said. 'Have you won the toss?'

'Yes,' I replied proudly.

'And are you going to bat?'

'Yes,' I said, even more proudly.

'And are you opening the batting?'

'Yes,' I said, puffing out my chest.

'In that case,' said the lady, 'I'll go into Hove to do my Sainsbury's shop before lunch!'

Dickie Bird:

I was still at school when I saw Walter Hammond play but I reckon he was probably the best player on all pitches who has ever lived. He played for Gloucestershire and England and, of course, he captained England.

For many years I umpired with Arthur Jepson – we were both on the first-class umpires list – and before that

Arthur used to play for Nottinghamshire. He told me this story about a match he played in against Gloucestershire at Bristol. He said, 'It's a true story, Dickie, because I bowled at Hammond, so I know it's true.'

Walter Hammond won the toss and decided to bat first. He said to Charlie Barnett, 'I want you to go in first.'

Charlie said, 'I'm not going in first. I'll go in at number three when the shine's off the ball.'

Hammond said, 'I'm captain. If you don't open the innings, you can go home.'

So they had an argument and after that Charlie Barnett had to go in first. He got out to the last ball before lunch for 99. He came back to the dressing room, threw down his bat and said to Walter Hammond, 'That's how you bat, you so-and-so.'

After lunch Hammond went in at number three and between lunch and tea – Arthur Jepson told me he bowled at him all afternoon – Walter Hammond scored more than 200. He came into the pavilion at teatime and he said to Charlie Barnett, 'That's how you bat, Charlie. *That's* how you bat!'

Barry Johnston:

Before he became a popular Hollywood character actor in the 1930s, Sir C. Aubrey Smith was captain of Sussex for three years and he even played in one Test for

England. He was known as 'Round the Corner' for his unusual bowling style and he was a founder-member of the Hollywood Cricket Club. He was playing cricket once in America when he dropped an easy catch and called for his butler to bring out his glasses. Soon afterwards he dropped another catch and exclaimed, 'The idiot brought my *reading* glasses!'

Later in his life Smith was very deaf and he was at a dinner party in Hollywood when the conversation around him became very animated. He guessed that they were talking about the merits of different sports, when in fact they were discussing homosexuality, and the other dinner guests were surprised when he suddenly remarked, 'Well, whatever you say, give me three stumps, a bat and a ball!'

BATSMEN

Brian Johnston:

Denis Compton was the vaguest man there has ever been. He never remembered a single invitation, never arrived on time, always forgot his box or his bat or his pads, but went out and made a hundred with everybody else's equipment.

Many years ago Middlesex were giving a birthday party for him, on his fiftieth birthday. Champagne corks were popping in the Middlesex office up at Lord's when the telephone rang and they said, 'It's for you, Denis.'

He went, and came back looking a bit rum.

'Well, who was it, Denis?' they said.

'It's my mother,' said Denis. 'She says I'm only forty-nine!'

Dickie Bird:

The first West Indian batsmen to capture the public's imagination were the famous 'W' trio of Walcott, Weekes and Worrell. Jim Laker, that great England off-spin bowler, regarded Everton de Courcy Weekes as the greatest of the three, but was always curious about how he had come by his first name. One day he plucked up the courage to ask him.

'Ah, well, you see,' explained the West Indian, 'my dad was a football nutter. At the time I was born, Everton were the cock of the walk in the English First Division. So he decided to call me after that team.'

Said Laker, 'It's a bloody good job he wasn't a fan of West Bromwich Albion!'

Simon Hughes:

During a county championship match between Middlesex and Yorkshire at Lord's, Geoffrey Boycott kept reminding everyone that it was his one thousandth innings in first-class 'crickit'. Angus Fraser bowled superbly in the match and got so frustrated with Boycott's playing and missing that he finally emitted an agonised, 'D'you want a bell in it, Grandad?'

'If tha can see so well, why doesn't tha bool at stoomps?' came the triumphant reply.

Michael Parkinson:

Harold Larwood once told me of a famous encounter with Don Bradman at Leeds during the Third Test of the 1930 Ashes series when the little man played one of his great innings. Harold said there was no doubt in his mind that Bradman was the greatest batsman to whom he ever bowled.

'We worked on the theory he was uneasy against the short-pitched ball early on,' said Harold. 'Maurice Tate got Archie Jackson and they were 2 for 1. I gave Bradman a short one first ball. He played at it and there was a nick. George Duckworth caught it. We thought we had him but the umpire didn't agree. Mind you, we got him out shortly after.'

'How many had he got?' I asked, walking blindfold into the trap.

'Three hundred and thirty-four,' replied Harold with a grin.

Dickie Bird:

Back in 1963 I played for Leicestershire and I always used to open the batting. We were due to play the tourists, the West Indies, at Grace Road but I was having a terrible time. I couldn't get a run. In fact, I was in the second team.

The Leicestershire selection committee – all thirty-nine of them – sat down to pick the team to play against the West Indies and they decided to bring me back into the team. That was a big mistake for a start, because I was in such terrible form.

That 1963 West Indies team was a great side. They had Rohan Kanhai, Basil Butcher, Seymour Nurse, Frank Worrell, the captain, and Garfield Sobers, the greatest all-round cricketer that I've ever seen. But they also had two great fast bowlers – Wesley Hall and Charlie Griffith.

I thought, 'Oh dear! I'm in terrible form and they've selected me to play against these two. Well, I'll get to the ground early tomorrow morning and have a look where we're playing – see what sort of pitch our groundsman has prepared.'

Now I'm always early, wherever I go. I arrived that Saturday at about seven o'clock in the morning and I couldn't get into the ground, all the gates were locked. So I threw my bags over the wall, climbed over and went out to the middle to have a look at the pitch.

When I saw it, I couldn't believe it. The groundsman had left the grass on and I thought, 'Oh no!' Two of the world's fastest bowlers and Garfield Sobers as first change – and he could bowl a bit, I can tell you – and I always went in first and took the new ball.

So when the groundsman arrived, I said, 'Hey! Get this grass shaved off, man. Make it as flat as you possibly can.'

He said, 'I'm not going to touch it. I want to see some excitement today!'

I said, 'Tha'll see some excitement if thy don't get this grass off.'

He said, 'I'm not touching it.'

So when our captain, Maurice Hallam, arrived, I said, 'Hey, Maurice, if you win the toss, shove the West Indies in to bat because I don't fancy going out there and playing against Charlie Griffith and Wes Hall.'

He said, 'No. Neither do I, not on here. I'll shove them in if I win the toss.'

I said, 'Don't forget.'

So the two captains went out, Frankie Worrell and Maurice Hallam. Up went the coin, down it came and, after all I'd told him, Maurice won the toss and decided to bat first. Now that was another big mistake. I thought, 'Well, I've got to go out there and do my best.' So I padded up and went out with Maurice Hallam to open the innings for Leicestershire.

In those days we didn't wear helmets and we didn't have big chest protectors or thigh pads. We had nothing like that. My 'thigh pad' was my handkerchief. I just kept thinking, 'I've got to face them,' took leg-stump guard from the umpire and prepared for the first ball from Wes Hall.

I watched him marking his run-up out at the Pavilion End and I thought, 'Where's he going?' I thought he might be going to move the sightscreen. But he wasn't. He was marking his run-up at the side of it. I looked in front of me and I couldn't see any fielders. I thought, 'That's funny. Where's his fielders?' I looked over my right shoulder and, thirty yards back, he'd got nine slips. I said, 'Are you playing with us?'

I thought, 'Well, I'll show him.' I saw Wesley Hall race in and he had this big gold medallion that was swinging in the breeze as he ran, and I didn't see anything else. I think I pushed forward, I don't know, I may have played back, but I saw nothing.

I looked up and all the West Indies players were running round him and hugging him. 'Well bowled, Wes! Well bowled!' I thought, 'Well bowled? That's funny.' Then I looked down and there were no off and middle stumps. I thought, 'Where did they go?' I looked over my right shoulder and I could see them many a mile past the wicket-keeper.

And I've often thought, if I'd taken off and middle, I don't think I'd be here today!

Barry Johnston:

On 31 December 1920 a young woman named Mrs Park was sitting in the VIP enclosure at the Melbourne Cricket Ground, watching the Second Test match against England and happily doing her knitting. At one point, she fumbled and dropped her ball of wool. She bent down to pick it up – and missed her husband's entire international career!

Roy Park, known as 'Little Doc', was a doctor by profession. He played for Victoria and was making his Test debut, batting at number three for Australia. He was bowled first ball by Harry Howell, who was also making his Test debut. Australia went on to win the match by an innings and 91 runs, so Park did not face another ball, and was never selected again. Years later he admitted he hadn't been to bed the night before the Test because he had been supervising a difficult birth.

The good Dr Park was bowled by the only ball he ever faced in international cricket!

Simon Hughes:

There are as many Geoffrey Boycott stories as he's played forward defensives, but this is my favourite. Mike Hendrick had been bowling some dastardly leg-cutters at our Geoffrey, none of which he could lay a bat on, but he kept up a gibing banter for most of the morning.

Hendrick (after an edge had gone between the slips): 'How many great bowlers *are* there in the world?'

Boycott (defiant): 'One less than tha thinks there are. Now, get back and bool.'

Hendrick (later, beating the bat): 'Has that bat got 'ole in it?'

Boycott: 'I'd put thee in mook and nettles if tha give me woon to reach.'

At length the mischievous umpire, Arthur Jepson, had had enough of this incessant rabbit and when Hendrick nipped one back into Boycott's pads and let out a half-hearted appeal, Jepson gave him out. Stunned and appalled by what appeared to be an outrageous injustice, Boycott marched off, muttering to the umpire as he passed, 'Hey, Arthur, what's happened to your guide dog?'

'I sacked it for yapping, same as I'm doing to you,' Jepson replied. 'Now piss off!'

Dickie Bird:

The Northamptonshire batsman David Steele was a member of the county side that won the Gillette Cup in 1976, just a year after England had successfully turned to him to help resist the fiery challenge of the West Indies' pacemen. David's proudest moments were when he played for his country. He would point to the three lions on his chest and say, 'You can't take that away.'

One thing he did not like was spending his money. Once, when I was umpiring a game in which he was playing, we had a bit of a natter between overs, and he told me, 'I went to the fair last night, Dickie, and I'm not very happy.'

I said, 'Why's that then, David? What happened?'

'Well,' he replied, 'I spent sixpence on the hoop-la and I didn't win a thing. I'm so disappointed!'

Martin Johnson:

In his early years with Leicestershire, there was no telling what kind of shambolic state David Gower would arrive in for breakfast, which led to his captain Ray Illingworth delivering him a 'smarten up' lecture. Gower's response was to turn up next morning wearing a dinner jacket and bow tie, but Illy was not quite sure about the joke.

'Bloody hell, Gower,' he inquired. 'Have you just come in or are you just going out?'

Brian Johnston:

When Bryan 'Bomber' Wells came in to bat for Nottinghamshire against the Australians at Trent Bridge in 1964, Neil Hawke was in devastating form. The umpire, ready to give him guard, said, 'What do you want, Bomber?'

To which Bomber replied, 'Help!'

A few years earlier, when Bomber was playing for Gloucestershire, he was batting one day with Sam Cook.

They got into a terrible tangle over a short single, with Sam just making the crease by hurling himself flat on the ground. As he lay there panting he shouted out to Bomber, 'Call!'

Bomber shouted back, 'Tails!'

Michael Parkinson:

The Don Bradman legend is built on stories underlining the prowess that set him apart from other men. There is, for instance, the tale of Bill Black, an off-spin bowler playing for Lithgow, in New South Wales, who on a memorable day in 1931 bowled Bradman for 52. The umpire was so excited that when the ball hit Bradman's wicket he called out, 'Bill, you've got him!'

The ball was mounted and given to Bill Black as proof that he dismissed the greatest batsman in the world.

Later that season Don Bradman again played against Bill Black. As the bowler marked out his run, Don said to the wicket-keeper, 'What sort of bowler is this fellow?'

The wicket-keeper, a mischievous fellow, like the rest of his tribe, replied, 'Don't you remember this bloke? He bowled you out a few weeks ago and has been boasting about it ever since.'

'Is that so?' said Bradman.

Two overs later Black pleaded with his skipper to be taken off. Bradman had hit him for 62 runs in two eight-ball overs. He made a hundred in three overs and finished with 256, including 14 sixes and 29 fours!

The other side to Bradman's genius is demonstrated by an encounter with George Macaulay, the feisty Yorkshire seam bowler, in 1930. It was Bradman's first tour of England and there was a popular rumour that the English wickets would sort him out. As an ardent subscriber to this theory, Macaulay couldn't wait to get at Bradman.

When Yorkshire played the Australians early in the tour, Macaulay demanded loudly of his captain, 'Let me have a go at this bugger.'

His first over was a maiden. Bradman then hit him for five fours in the second over and took 16 from the third. A spectator yelled, 'George, tha' should have kept thi' bloody trap shut!'

Colin Ingleby-Mackenzie:

I had entertained Denis Compton to lunch during a Test match at Lord's. After lunch we strolled round the ground and behind the pavilion we noticed Geoffrey Boycott and David Gower in a keen discussion. They were discussing how many first-class hundreds each had made. Geoffrey said, 'I told you I've made more than you!'

Denis Compton quickly retorted, 'And thank God I've only seen three of them!'

Graeme Fowler:

I was with Derek Pringle, Derek Randall, Richard Ellison and Dickie Bird, and we were telling cricket stories. Derek Randall, known as 'Arkle', is brilliant – a very funny man – and the rest of us were trying to get him going. We started talking about the number of runs people had got in their careers, because someone mentioned Dennis Amiss, who has got a phenomenal amount, over 40,000, which is ridiculous. Then someone said, 'How many has Boycott got?' and that was answered.

Then I asked, 'Arkle, how many have you got?'

He replied, '16,526 – and four of them were leg byes!'

Martin Johnson:

Ray Illingworth has a belief in his own ability that has occasionally had people in fits of helpless giggles. He was, for instance, never out when he was batting. On one occasion, having missed a particularly horrible slog, he returned to the dressing room and claimed that the bowler's grunt in his delivery stride made him think it was the umpire calling a no-ball. On another, when there seemed no possible excuse even for him, he said, 'Would you believe it? Bloody umpire gave me t'wrong guard.'

His reputation as a captain was for erring on the defensive side, which is again in keeping with his thrifty nature. He knows all the best fish and chip shops in Yorkshire, and which bars in Torremolinos give you non-watered-down rum at the cheapest prices. Once, as captain of Leicestershire, he negotiated 10 per cent off the team's hotel bill because he couldn't get any sausages for breakfast!

Dickie Bird:

Out of all the great players I've seen, if I had to pick a batsman to bat for my life, I'd go for Geoffrey Boycott. He was probably the best self-made player in the history of the game. Mind you, there were times in Test matches when I was umpiring and he was batting and he was there, blocking every ball, and I had to say to myself, 'Come on, get a grip of yourself, Dickie. Get a grip. Don't let him put you to sleep!'

I was told once that to make the best Yorkshire pudding you had to have a very slow batter – and Boycott springs immediately to mind.

Boycott had one bad habit – he ran people out. Me included. He once ran me out playing for Barnsley and I'd have had the biggest collection they'd ever had at Barnsley Cricket Club. I was on 49, there were three thousand people in the ground, and I hit this ball to deep midwicket. I shouted, 'Come two,' and ran down the pitch, and Boycott said, 'Keep running . . . into the pavilion!'

One man ran Boycott out. It was in a Test match in New Zealand. The England captain, Mike Brearley, had returned home with a broken arm and Geoffrey Boycott had been appointed as captain. England were playing New Zealand at Christchurch and the New Zealand captain left England a very good declaration. Bob Willis, the England vice-captain, called a meeting in the England dressing room as Boycott and Brian Rose were padding up to go out and open the innings for England.

Bob Willis said, 'Lads, we're going for these runs because we can win this Test match. This is a tremendous declaration. Now then, Geoffrey, I want you to play a few shots.'

Boycott said, 'Huh! I shall play me own game. Ain't nobody gonna tell me how I'm gonna play. I shall be a hundred and twenty not out at close of play.'

Bob Willis said, 'I want you to get out there and get on with it, because we can win this Test match.'

Boycott and Rose went out and opened the innings for England. Brian Rose was out after about an hour and Derek Randall went in next, but Boycott had put England well behind the clock. So Bob Willis called another meeting in the England dressing room. He said, 'Gentlemen, I want a volunteer to pad up and go in next, if Randall gets out, and run Boycott out!'

Ian Botham said, 'I volunteer!'

He said, 'Right, Both. If Randall gets out, you go in next.'

Well, Randall got out and Botham went in, and as he left the England dressing room all the England lads said, 'Good luck, Both!'

He said, 'Leave it to me.' Botham got out to the middle and he had a meeting with Boycott. He said, 'Geoffrey, instructions from the England dressing room: you have put us well behind the clock and you've got to play a few shots. You've got to get on with it.'

'I shall play me own game. There's no one telling me how I'm gonna play.'

Botham said, 'I'm telling you.'

'Well, there's nobody's telling me. I shall be 120 not out.'

Botham said, 'Oh, will you?'

Botham got down to face his first delivery. In came the bowler, Botham pushed the ball to cover point and shouted to Boycott, 'Come one!' Boycott, head down, charged down the wicket and nearly reached Botham's end, but Botham was still sat on his bat. He said, 'Sorry, Geoffrey, I'm not coming.' Boycott turned, tried to get back, but was run out by half the length of the field.

Boycott has hardly spoken to Botham since that day!

Fred Trueman:

In his old age, Sir Donald Bradman retained a wicked sense of humour. He was once asked by a newspaperman, 'How do you think you would have fared against today's bowlers, Sir Donald? Your career average was ninety-nine in Tests; what do you think it would have been against modern bowling and field-placing?'

Bradman pondered the point for a moment, then replied, 'I think I might have averaged about thirty-eight or thirty-nine perhaps.'

The reporter was shaken. 'Do you mean,' he asked breathlessly, 'that you regard today's bowling as so much better?'

'Oh, no,' said Sir Donald. 'What you asked was what do I think I would have averaged *today*, and the answer is thirty-eight or thirty-nine. Don't forget that *today* I'm eighty-four years old!'

Richie Benaud:

I like the story about Colin Cowdrey when he was flown out to Australia as an additional batsman in 1974, after Dennis Amiss and John Edrich suffered broken bones in the First Test in Brisbane.

In the Second Test at the WACA in Perth, Cowdrey batted number three and went in after Brian Luckhurst was caught by Ashley Mallett in the gully off Max Walker for 27, with the score 44. It was a perfect day and sixteen thousand spectators watched Cowdrey walk to the centre. The crowd was lively because they were watching some very fast bowling from Jeff Thomson and Dennis Lillee. No one said a word to Colin.

After a couple of overs, as 'Thommo' was walking back past the non-striker's end, Colin took a pace towards him, smiled and said politely, 'Good morning, my name's Cowdrey!'

Sometimes you need a sense of humour. In the same game David Lloyd made 49 in the first innings and announced to his fellow players that he could play Thomson with his prick. In the second innings he had made 17 when Thommo got one to rear and the ball smashed his protective box to pieces. When they had air-lifted him back to the England dressing room his first agonising words through gritted teeth to solicitous team-mates were, 'See, told you I could.'

TEST MATCH SPECIAL

Brian Johnston:

I was very lucky to get into *Test Match Special*. I did twenty-four years on the television up to 1970 and then they got fed up with all my bad jokes and thought they would get in some Test players to do the commentary, which was sensible, because they do it very well.

Luckily, I went straight into *Test Match Special* and it's a lovely programme to do, because we go and watch cricket, like anyone else, with friends. If someone says, 'Have a little drink,' we might have a small one, or if someone has heard a good story, we might tell it. I hope we never miss a ball, but we have *fun* and that's the great thing to me about cricket.

We have got one or two eccentric people in the commentary box. What about Blowers, 'my dear old thing' – Henry Blofeld? When he was aged eighteen, Henry was one of the best wicket-keepers at Eton anyone had ever seen. He was captain of the Eton XI, but one day he rode a bicycle out of the playing fields into Datchet Lane and he was knocked over by a Women's Institute bus.

36

The ambulance took him away and he had an operation on his brain. He got a Blue at Cambridge later! So he was all right, but I think that accident gave him what I call 'busitis', because doing a commentary at Lord's he'll say, 'That ball goes through to the wicket-keeper. I can see a number eighty-two bus approaching . . . a Green Line bus . . . a double-decker bus . . .' He has buses on the brain! At The Oval once he said, 'I can see a good-looking bus!'

If a pigeon flies by, it's always 'a thoughtful-looking pigeon'. At Headingley, he said, 'I can see a butterfly walking across the pitch . . . and what's more, it's got a limp!'

He gets terribly excited. Someone dropped an easy catch and he said, 'A very easy catch. Very easy catch. It's a catch he'd have caught ninety-nine times out of a thousand!'

Henry Blofeld:

My first Test match in 1974 was not without incident because there was a lot of rain. You know how on *Test Match Special* we prattle on when it rains and we never hand back to the studio. We talk about absolutely anything. I was rather frightened about doing this at first but Brian Johnston was marvellous at it. If there were forty-eight hours in a day he would never have drawn breath and I don't know how he did it.

On the second day after lunch there was no play and Brian said, 'Let's bring Blowers in.' I'd thought of a few things to say, so I sat down and Johnners got up. I put my head to the windscreen, so to speak, and I started off. I rattled on for about ten minutes and I thought I was doing awfully well. I was telling them about this, that and the other, and I thought it was really sparkling stuff. Then I ran out of steam and I thought, goodness me, I need a bit of help.

So I stopped and looked to my right – I was sitting in the left-hand end of the box – and there should have been about four people there. To my absolute horror there was no one there at all. Not a soul. There was just a piece of paper almost in front of me in BJ's writing, and written on it was: CARRY ON UNTIL SIX-THIRTY AND DON'T FORGET TO HAND BACK TO THE STUDIO.

It was then about two-thirty.

Suddenly flat panic set in and I couldn't get any sense out at all. This seemed to go on forever until they all came tumbling back into the box, howling with laughter. But what Johnners had been saying to me in the nicest possible way, and doing it with great tact and humour, was, 'Hey, watch it, you're playing a team game,' and I never forgot that. It really taught me a lesson!

Brian Johnston:

We receive thousands of letters at *Test Match Special* but the writers don't always understand us. Some of the letters are marvellous and there are two I always keep on file.

Once I said that Freddie Titmus was coming on to bowl and I added, 'He's got two short-legs, one of them square.' A woman wrote in, 'No need to be rude about people's disabilities!'

On another occasion Ken Barrington had made 111 and I said, 'He's batting very well now. He's a bit lucky – he was dropped when two.' In came a letter saying, 'Mothers should be more careful with their babies!'

Henry Blofeld:

Another thing that Johnners did during my first Test match nearly ended my entire broadcasting career. It's something I shall never forget. On one of the days when there was some cricket, Tony Greig was bowling to Sunil Gavaskar, the Indian opening batsman.

Johnners was on the air and he said, 'Here comes Tony Greig now from the Warwick Road End, this great gangling tall chap, he's up to the wicket now and he bowls and Gavaskar plays forward, and that one runs down to Hendrick at mid-on. Hendrick picks it up, looks at the ball, polishes it and throws it back to Greig, who now strides back down this long run of his, polishing the ball on his right thigh. He gets to the end of his run, he turns, sees Gavaskar is ready, and in he comes again. He's up there, he bowls, Gavaskar plays forward, and history repeats itself. The ball rolls down to Hendrick at mid-on, who picks it up this time and throws it straight back to Greig and now, to ring the changes as he walks back, Greig polishes his left ball.'

At which point the entire commentary box fell about, including dear old BJ, and the only thing he was able to say – it was the last ball of the over – was, 'and now, after a word from Trevor Bailey, it will be Henry Blofeld.'

The box was heaving, Bill Frindall was snorting, and how I got through the next over I will never know!

Barry Johnston:

One of the main summarisers on *Test Match Special* throughout the 1970s and 1980s was Trevor Bailey, the former Essex and England all-rounder. He was a useful man to have in the commentary box because, unlike almost everyone else, he was able to keep a straight face. His nickname was 'Boil', which led to an unfortunate slip of the tongue when Brian Johnston introduced him one day, announcing, 'I'm joined by the Balls . . . I mean, the Boil!'

During another Test match there was a discussion in the box about whether a particular captain should make the other side bat again the following day and how he would have the evening to think about it. Brian turned to Bailey and asked innocently, 'Have you ever slept on it overnight, Trevor?'

There was a collective gasp from the rest of the commentary box followed by silence on the air as Brian struggled to control himself. Trevor had to step into the breach and for the next three minutes he talked about the weather, the pitch and anything else he could think of, until the others were able to speak.

Bill Frindall:

Henry Blofeld has been able to offer many descriptions that stick in the memory, whether one wants them to or not. My favourite is: 'I can see a lady with the most enormous pair of binoculars!'

For several seasons Blowers relied on me to scrutinise any notes or emails that were passed to him. In fact, I became his censor. Brian Johnston, David Lloyd, Jon Agnew, and even our producer, have competed in a prolonged campaign to get him to read out the most blatant *double entendres*. Frequently they have succeeded in bypassing me by slipping them under his pile of post from the far side, hidden under *bona fide* notes instructing him to hand over for the shipping forecast.

One slipped through the net just before lunch on a Saturday at Edgbaston and involved Evesham Cricket Club. The club asked us to pass an urgent message to their scorer, who was sitting in the Eric Hollies stand. Apparently, his deputy had been taken ill and they needed him back.

The note advised that the scorer, Richard Head, would be listening to *TMS*. 'Dick's a shy man,' the note continued, 'and he wouldn't want to hear his name read out over the ground's public address system. Please help us get him back for our afternoon match.'

Blowers dutifully read out the note and added, 'So, if you're listening Dick Head, please hurry back to Evesham!'

Fred Trueman:

Johnners once received a letter at *Test Match Special* that even he deemed was inadvisable to read over the airwaves. It came after a streaker had been led away by a policeman who diplomatically placed his helmet over the streaker's most treasured possessions. With an innocence that matched Brian's, the lady correspondent asked, 'Could you please tell us – what was the policeman's hat size?'

Henry Blofeld:

A big problem we have in the commentary box is the awful one of spoonerisms, which absolutely haunt me. I remember one time at Lord's in the early 1990s, when India were playing and Gooch scored 333 and then a hundred in the second innings. I was on the air when he got his three-hundredth run. Ravi Shastri, the left-arm spinner, was bowling and Gooch tickled him round the corner and, of course, there was an absolute crescendo of noise.

I was describing this and I thought I'd stop talking and just let the noise carry on. Then I thought something vaguely Churchillian was required, so metaphorically I put my thumbs in my braces and I said, 'Never before in the history of this great ground of ours have so many runs been scored by one batsman in the same innings in a Test match,' and I got rather a taste for it.

Sadly, I had another go at it and I said, 'Never before in the history of this great ground of ours has a cloud *crapped* like this one!'

Bill Frindall:

Brian Johnston was an enthusiastically active president of the Metro Club for the Blind and his regular plugs for the Primary Club on *Test Match Special* greatly boosted that famous charity's membership. One of

Johnners' favourite stories involved his interview with a blind parachutist.

Brian said, 'I am full of admiration for what you do. Incredibly courageous. But how on earth do you know when you are about to land?'

The blind man replied, 'Oh, that's no problem! The lead on the guide dog goes slack!'

Henry Blofeld:

One of the things we like to do on *Test Match Special* is an interview during the lunch interval on Saturdays, called 'A View from the Boundary', where the great and the good, who've got an interest in cricket, come into the commentary box for a chat. In 2005 the actor Nigel Havers came in to be my guest during the Edgbaston Test match. After we'd talked for about a quarter of an hour, I said to him, 'Tell me, Nigel, do you have any trouble with sex scenes?'

He said, rather quickly, 'What do you mean?'

I said, 'Oh, nothing really, I just thought you might have found them rather embarrassing.'

'Oh, yes,' he said. 'I thought I was going to, but I didn't. The reason was that before I did my first sex scene on a movie I ran into Roger Moore, who gave me a great piece of advice. He said that before you embark upon a sex scene you've always got to apologise to the girl, before you even go into the first rehearsal, and you

make two apologies. First of all you say to her, "My dear, I apologise heartily if I get aroused during the course of this," and then you add, "but I apologise even more if I *don't* get aroused!" '

Brian Johnston:

Another great character on *Test Match Special* was Don Mosey, who was known as 'The Alderman'. He was talking about David Gower at Headingley in 1989 when he said, 'This is David Gower's one hundredth Test match and I'll tell you something. He's reached his one hundredth Test in fewer Test matches than any other player!'

Henry Blofeld:

I never commentated with Rex Alston but his finest hour in the cricket world came in 1962 and it's hysterically funny. Whenever I feel badly in need of a glass of champagne and I haven't got one, I put on a tape of this, and it's jolly nearly as good.

In 1962 when Pakistan came to England for the second time, they had a player whose name was a commentator's nightmare. You know how their players usually have two names, like Imran Khan or Javed Miandad. Well, this chap's second name was Hussain, like the bloke in Baghdad but unrelated, I think. The first name was the problem. It was Afaq. Now pronounced quickly, with the wrong pronunciation, or slowly, with the right pronunciation, or simply muddled through, people listening around England could get quite the wrong impression of what was actually going on. So commentators had to be fairly careful.

In those days, the commentary boxes for television and radio were on the first-floor balcony in the pavilion. Brian Johnston presided over television and Rex Alston was on the radio. Rex was always known as 'Balston', for the very simple reason that he got so many things wrong, and Johnners loved to pull his leg. So, about half an hour before the start, Johnners went into the radio box and said, 'Morning, Balston, I see Afaq's not playing.'

Rex said, 'Oh, Johnners, I wish you'd never mentioned his name. I shall never get it out of my mind all day.' But as he went out of the box, Johnners kept muttering, 'Afaq, Afaq, Afaq.' Well, Rex tried awfully hard before lunch, and he never thought about the name at all. He had a completely teetotal lunch, in order not to think about it before tea, but the problem started after tea. He was doing the final twenty-minute session of the day, there were about eight or nine minutes to go, and in his lovely modulated voice he said, 'England have had a really marvellous day here at Lord's. There has hardly been a cloud in the sky. Barry Knight is playing a very useful innings and I can tell you now that Javed Burki, the Pakistan captain, has made a gambler's last throw. We've got a change of bowling and we're going to see Afaq to Knight at the Nursery End . . . Oh! What am I saying? He's not even playing!'

Brian Johnston:

To me, John Arlott did more to spread the gospel of cricket than anybody. That marvellous Hampshire burr with the slightly gravelly voice, especially in the years after the war, went all around the world, from igloos in Iceland to the outback in Australia.

Every time you heard him, you could smell bat oil and new-mown grass, and picture white flannels on a village green with a pub and a church. He could really conjure up cricket for you, and he was very good at painting a picture with words, because before he became a commentator, he was a poet.

To show you how quick he was, and witty, and how well he did it – there was a chap called Asif Masood, who bowled for Pakistan in 1962. Bill Frindall says I once called him Massif Ahsood. (I don't think I did, but never mind!) This chap ran up with bent knees, very low down, and the first time John saw him, he said, 'Reminds me of Groucho Marx chasing a pretty waitress!'

Another famous example happened when England were in South Africa in 1948/49. George Mann, the

England captain, was clean bowled by 'Tufty' M.
the South African slow left-hander, and John sai
'Another example of Mann's inhumanity to Mann!'

Fred Trueman:

John Arlott was never at a loss to find the right words
to describe a situation for those who could not see it.
Many of his descriptive phrases have passed into both
broadcasting and cricket legend:

'Umpire Fagg, his face like Walt Disney's idea of what
a grandfather should look like.'

On a characteristically long and dogged innings from
Geoffrey Boycott: 'No man is an island, but he has
batted as though he was a particularly long peninsula.'

'Dennis Lillee begins his run-up; black hair lounging
on his shoulders like an anaesthetised cocker spaniel.'

'Bev Congdon remains at the crease to frustrate
England, like some lingering, unloved guest at a party.'

'Charlotte Rampling is in the crowd. Charlotte
Rampling. Her name to me suggestive of an active
verb.'

Henry Blofeld:

You never quite knew what was coming next with Johnners. He was dynamite in the box. There was a lovely moment at Headingley in 1976, when they were rather against intruders because, the year before, the George Davis fan club had dug up the pitch. George Davis was a London minicab driver who had been wrongly convicted of armed robbery and he was eventually freed. Funnily enough, when they rearrested him two years later, the High Court judge who sent him to prison was none other than my brother, so at least the family honour was saved!

But anyway, they were dead against intruders the following year and everything went swimmingly until just after lunch on Saturday when, from the position of the old, old pavilion, the one that Lord Hawke used to walk out from – there are two old pavilions at Headingley now – a little black-and-white dachshund cantered out into the middle. It was determined to go to the Kirkstall Lane End, for some reason, and Brian was on the air.

He said, 'Well, we've got an intruder. A little black-and-white dachshund. He's a chirpy little chap. He's making a beeline for the Kirkstall Lane End. He's wrong-footed cover point, he's sold gully a dummy and, goodness me, he's now in the middle of the pitch. He's scratching away with his right front paw. Do you know, I think he's going to spend a penny. So too does umpire Tom Spencer. He's got one of the bowler's sleeveless jerseys and he's shooing it away. It's quite a promising little bullfight. But I can tell you at home that this dachshund is a fast bowler – and the reason I know he's a fast bowler is because he's got four short-legs and his balls swing both ways!'

Brian Johnston:

Luckily for me, I wasn't on air when the first streaker came on at Lord's. Remember the male streaker in 1975? He ran on and did the splits over the stumps. Fortunately, John Arlott was on and he described it brilliantly, wittily and gently. He said everything that needed saying; he didn't hide what he could see but he did it in a way that I couldn't possibly have done. I'd have got the sack, but he didn't.

It was interesting because Alan Knott was the non-striker at the far end. This chap came from the Pavilion End and did the splits over the stumps and then ran down towards the Nursery End. I said, 'What was it like out there, Knotty?'

'Oh,' he said, 'it really was most extraordinary. It's the first time I've ever seen two balls come down the pitch at the same time!'

Henry Blofeld:

John Arlott's choice of adjectives was supreme. 'The big, burly Bedser striding in from the Pavilion End' conjured up the perfect picture of a genial tidal wave, just as 'the balcony on the first floor of the pavilion with the portly iron railing' left one in no doubt as to the shape of this particular balcony at Old Trafford. It perfectly described a railing that bulges towards the base and looks like every elderly tummy one has ever seen.

It was at the Lord's Test match in 1975 that England's first streaker appeared, a merchant seaman from Marylebone who was enjoying his shore leave more than he should have done. Happily, Arlott was on the air most memorably to immortalise the moment:

'We've got a freaker! Not very shapely . . . and it's masculine. And I would think it's seen the last of its cricket for the day. The police are mustered; so are the cameramen and Greg Chappell. He's being embraced by a blond policeman and this may be his last public appearance, but what a splendid one. He's now being marched down in a final exhibition past at least eight thousand people in the Mound Stand, some of whom, perhaps, have never seen anything quite like this before!'

Brian Johnston:

There was a Yorkshireman who used to send me rhymes about cricket and he sent me one about the Lord's streaker:

> *He ran on in his birthday attire*
> *And he set all the ladies afire*
> *When he came to the stumps*
> *He misjudged his jumps*
> *Now he sings in the Luton Girls Choir!*

Barry Johnston:

Don Mosey was the worst giggler in the commentary box and he shared with Brian Johnston an acute sense of the ridiculous that could swiftly reduce them both to helpless giggles. One day a listener sent in a copy of the Israeli Cricket Association's handbook. Brian was sitting at the back of the commentary box, flipping idly through the book, when he came to the record section. His eye fell on the pair who had made the highest tenth-wicket stand for Israel, Solly Katz and Benny Wadwaker.

He tried desperately not to make a noise, but soon stifled laughter exploded from the back of the box. Don Mosey was on air at the time and, without having any idea what was funny, found himself overcome by Brian's infectious high-pitched giggle and was completely unable to continue!

Brian Johnston:

We have this funny thing in the commentary box about chocolate cake. It is silly, really, but someone sent me a cake once for my birthday and, perhaps unwisely, I said on the radio, 'Thank you very much for that delicious chocolate cake.'

Since then, they have arrived in droves. Of course, we played a silly trick on Alan McGilvray a few years ago. Incidentally, I think Alan McGilvray was the least biased and the fairest of all commentators. He was very good and he knew his cricket, because he captained New South Wales in the 1930s, when people such as Jack Fingleton and Bill O'Reilly were under him, and Don Bradman on occasion.

So he knew his cricket, but he didn't always understand our jokes. At Lord's, several years ago, I had cut some cake into slices on the desk alongside me and I was commentating when I saw him come in. I pointed to the cake and he nodded. I went on yap yapping away as he took a slice. 'That ball just goes off the edge of the bat and drops in front of first slip . . .' I watched Alan put it in his mouth and I said, 'We'll ask Alan McGilvray if he thought it was a catch.' He went *pfffft*. There were crumbs everywhere!

CHARACTERS

Henry Blofeld:

Colin Milburn, known to everyone as 'Ollie', was in the same league as P.G. Wodehouse's Right Honourable friend who looked as if he had been poured into his clothes and had forgotten to say 'When!' Fat men are often naturally humorous and Milburn always seemed to be the ideal chap to audition for the job of Stan Laurel's partner if ever another had been needed.

Milburn's figure raised a few eyebrows when he first joined Northamptonshire. They sent him on training runs with the rest of the team, but he was just not built to run a long way. After about half a mile the others had left him behind, so he thumbed a lift on a milk float and sailed past the rest of the team a bit farther up the road!

On another occasion, Keith Andrew, his county captain, suggested that Colin should try to do something about his weight, and also get some more hundreds.

'Why don't you drink halves instead of pints?' Andrew asked. Milburn made 150 that day and it was only about halfway through the afternoon.

'What are you going to drink then, Colin?' Andrew asked him.

Quick as a flash he said, 'Two halves, please, guv!'

Fred Trueman:

Charles Bowmar Harris was well into the veteran stage when I first encountered him – he was over forty. I was under twenty – but I knew *of* him, of course, as everyone in the game knew of the practical joker and genial eccentric who had been Nottinghamshire's opening batsman since 1928.

Jim Laker used to tell how Charlie stopped a fast bowler in full cry in his approach to the wicket with the explanation, 'You have an extra fieldsman in the gully.' The whole game was held up for an investigation to be made and it was then discovered that Harris had placed his false teeth on the ground in roughly the place gully would stand.

No one escaped Charlie's droll humour – and no one resented it. One day he was batting against Surrey when he put a dolly catch into the air. As three fieldsmen plus wicket-keeper edged forward – all with an equal chance of making the catch – Charlie trotted quietly by and shouted, 'Mine.' Everyone stopped and the ball fell gently to earth!

Henry Blofeld:

Ollie Milburn came as a breath of fresh air for English cricket and it was cruel that, after playing in only nine Test matches for England, he was involved in a car crash in 1969 that cost him the use of one eye and damaged the other. For a time he tried bravely to overcome this enormous handicap and his humour never left him.

He was playing against Derbyshire with only one eye and was bowling. As he ran in to deliver one ball, he suddenly stopped and shouted that his eye had fallen out. Everyone searched around the crease and the umpire found it. Milburn took out his handkerchief, gave the glass eye a rub, shoved it back in and, after a good chortle, finished the over.

Brian Johnston:

Brian Close was one of the bravest cricketers I've ever seen. Remember him batting against the West Indies in 1963, against Hall and Griffith? Rather than risk giving a catch, he bared his breast at them and let the ball hit him. You could see the maker's name all over him. He was very brave and, of course, he always fielded near in at short-leg.

There's a story about when Yorkshire were playing Gloucestershire and Martin Young was batting; Ray

Illingworth was bowling and Close was right in there at forward short-leg.

For once, Ray bowled a bit of a short ball outside the off stump, which Martin Young pulled and he got Close above his right eye. The ball ballooned up over Jimmy Binks, the wicket-keeper, and into the hands of Phil Sharpe at first slip – caught!

Blood was pouring down Close's face. It didn't worry him, he just wiped it away, and fielded for about another ten minutes. Then the lunch interval came and he walked back – blood still pouring down – and as he went in, one of the members said, 'Mr Close, you mustn't stand as near as that. It's very dangerous. What would have happened if it had hit you slap between the eyes?'

He said, 'He'd have been caught at cover!'

Henry Blofeld:

I would have paid any money in the world to see W.G. Grace. He was obviously a bit of a crook, but he must have been a fine cricketer. There are lots of lovely stories about him but the one I like most of all is when Neville Cardus was talking to one of the old Gloucestershire professionals who'd played with WG and he asked him, 'Do you think that WG ever cheated?'

This old Gloucestershire professional looked at Neville

Cardus and said, 'The Old Man cheat? Why, 'e were much too clever for that!'

The other one I like is when he was bowled and the ball just flicked his off bail. The Doctor leant down, picked up the bail and put it back on the stumps, and said, 'Windy day, umpire, isn't it?'

The umpire said, 'Yes it is, Dr Grace, and mind it don't blow your hat off on the way back to the pavilion!'

Dickie Bird:

W.G. Grace was so feared by the umpires of his day that some hardly dared to give him out, and he bent the rules quite unashamedly on more than one occasion. During one innings in a county match he lofted the ball skywards into the outfield, ran one, and, as he turned for the second, noticed a fielder nicely positioned for the catch. He immediately declared the innings – with the ball still in the air – to avoid being given out and having his average spoiled. He claimed that the catch had been taken after close of play!

Henry Blofeld:

There are plenty of other stories about WG, usually constructed around his inbuilt reluctance to leave the crease when the umpire had indicated otherwise. When he ticked off umpires for giving him out, saying, 'They've come to see me bat, not you umpire,' he was right. He was an institution and the huge crowds came hoping they would see him add to his mountain of runs.

His career as a doctor inevitably came second, but he was still much loved by his patients as he went about his business in a brisk, jovial and efficient way. After a difficult maternity case, he is said to have told his friends, 'Well, the baby's dead and I don't think there's much hope for the mother, but I do believe I shall pull the father through.'

On another occasion, when instructing a mother to put her children, both of whom had high temperatures, to bed, he said, 'There's no need to call me unless they get up to 210 for 2 before lunch!'

David Lloyd:

Jack Simmons was 27, and a qualified draughtsman with Lancashire County Council, before he came full-time into county cricket, but it's fair to say he made up for lost time. He went on to chair the Lancashire commit-tee, and the club, plainly, is his life. The stories of his eating habits are legion. They are also all true.

I took him home once after a day's play and he asked to be dropped at a chippy, called Jack's, 500 yards from his home. Once he'd bought his fish and chips, he sat down on the wall outside to eat them. It was raining, he lived a block or so away and I was still there waiting to chauffeur him, so I asked what seemed the natural question. 'Why don't you take them home, Jack, eat them in your own kitchen?'

He looked alarmed. He said, 'If I take these home, Jackie'll not make me any supper!'

Fred Trueman:

Charlie Harris once dived to take a catch off Harold Butler and rolled around the ground in agony, claiming he had broken a bone. It was, in fact, nothing more than a dislocation – painful enough, I suppose – and Charlie was taken to hospital for a precautionary X-ray.

When told it was a minor injury and that the dislocation was to be put back into position, he enquired, nervously, 'Will it hurt?'

'Not much,' he was told, and the sleeve was rolled up ready for the simple operation. Charlie took a towel, rolled it up tightly and clenched it between his teeth as the collarbone was put back – and he screamed!

A senior nurse, who was, as it happened, an ardent Notts supporter, reproached him severely. 'There's a nineteen-year-old girl just down the corridor who gave birth to twins this morning,' she told him, 'and she didn't make half so much noise as you.'

'Aye,' replied Charlie, 'but just you try putting 'em back!'

Henry Blofeld:

There may never be a more humorous cricketer than Patsy Hendren. Patsy was a natural clown and wherever he played, he brought joy and happiness to the crowds and to all but the most curmudgeonly of those with or against whom he played.

What enabled Hendren to play the measured fool as he did was his brilliant batting. Only two others, Sir Jack Hobbs and Frank Woolley, have scored more first-class runs than Hendren, and Hobbs is the only one who has scored more than his 170 centuries.

When he was fielding on the boundary he developed the habit, which always got him a laugh, of chasing a ball in the outfield and bending down as if to pick it up when he was still ten yards short of it. It was no surprise if the batsman fell for it and refused a safe third run.

Hendren loved practical jokes. He tried one at the end of his career on his Middlesex captain, Walter Robins. When Robins was batting, he used to charge down the wicket to the spinners and if he missed the ball he would carry on walking towards the pavilion without a backward glance. Once when Hendren was the non-striker,

Robins rushed out of his ground to a spinner, missed and was about to continue to walk when Hendren yelled, 'Look out, he's missed it!'

Robins spun round and threw himself headlong on a muddy pitch to get his bat into his crease. The crowd roared and Robins got up, brushed himself down and then saw that the wicket was broken and the keeper, Harry Elliott, was grinning broadly and tossing the ball from hand to hand!

David Lloyd:

When Lancashire were playing at Blackpool one year, Jack Simmons booked a table in the local fish restaurant. The curious thing was that he didn't book it for dinner but for lunch – on a playing day. I've seldom seen him move so fast as when the bails were lifted for the interval – he was away in his car, with a couple of other players in tow, and I'm told he demolished two specials, pudding, chips and peas with fish on top, and still got back for the first ball of the afternoon.

Occasionally, he didn't even make it. Southport always put on home-made gooseberry and cherry pies for pudding at lunchtime and when the bell went for us to take the field one day, he'd just started on a full one. For an over, Lancashire fielded with ten men. Then Jack emerged from the tent, licking his lips, the cat that got the cream.

He'd often stand at slip with a biscuit in his top pocket, just to keep him going, and he once justified eating two huge apple pies by saying, 'They said I was to eat a lot of fruit!'

Unsurprisingly, Jack Simmons was a very poor pre-season trainer, especially when it came to the five-mile run that would often complete our session in those days. He was once spotted climbing down from a lorry at the gates of Old Trafford, having tailed himself off from the rest of us and convinced the driver he was lost!

Brian Johnston:

On one occasion Patsy Hendren was fielding on the boundary by the famous Hill on the Sydney Cricket Ground. The batsman hit the ball high in the air towards him. As it soared higher and higher into the air a raucous voice from the Hill shouted, 'Patsy, if you miss the catch, you can sleep with my sister.'

Later Patsy was asked what he had done. 'Oh,' he replied, 'as I hadn't seen his sister, I caught the ball!'

Graeme Fowler:

Steve O'Shaughnessy, the Lancashire all-rounder, is very talented. But he speaks before he thinks, and often acts before he has worked out what he is doing. That can be very funny – he is a master of spoonerisms and *non sequiturs*. For instance, a woman came into a pub where we were. She had obviously just come back from Majorca or wherever, since she had this beautiful, deep tan, and Shauny asked her, 'Are you a sunship worper?'

On the same day a kid asked him for his autograph, proferring a cigarette packet. Shauny said, 'Have you no paper? I'm not signing that pag facket!'

Once a girl rang the dressing room for him when he wasn't there. He was given the message – she would ring back later, but didn't leave a name.

'Oh.' Pause. 'Was she a blonde?'

On another occasion he was out playing golf with Pete Lever, and Pete, who is a keen bird-watcher, said, 'Listen, that's a green woodpecker.'

'Oh.' Pause. 'How can you tell it's green?'

Dickie Bird:

Two of the greatest characters to have left the Test match scene are Ian Botham and Allan Lamb. I was glad when they went, really, because they were always taking the mickey out of me during a Test match. Once I came in from square-leg to stand at the bowler's end and Ian Botham had set off a pile of Chinese firecrackers behind the stumps!

In a Test match at Trent Bridge, England were playing the West Indies. England had lost two wickets very quickly and Allan Lamb came out to bat at number four. He walked down the members' enclosure at Trent Bridge, out on to the middle, and he came towards me at square-leg. I thought, 'What's he coming over to me for at square-leg?' I said, 'Lamby, we're playing over there!'

He said, 'I want *you*.'

I thought, 'Oh dear,' and I asked, 'What do you want, man?'

He said, 'When I padded up and put my gloves on, I rushed to get out at the fall of the wicket and I forgot to take my mobile phone out of my pocket.'

I said, 'What do you want me to do with that?'

He replied, 'I want you to put it in your pocket and if it rings, I want you to answer it.'

'We're in the middle of a Test match, man,' I said. 'You'll get me shot.'

He said, 'Shove it in your pocket and if it rings, I'm expecting some important messages.'

Lamby went off and took guard off my colleague and soon he was playing away. Then after about five overs, the phone started to ring in my pocket.

'Hello?' I said, 'Who's there?'

'This is Ian Botham, ringing from the dressing room.'

'What do you want?' I said. 'I've enough problems out here.'

'Tell that fellow Lamb to play a few shots or get out!'

I said, 'Lamby . . . it's for you!'

Henry Blofeld:

One of the best stories involving Patsy Hendren happened in 1929, when Alf Gover played for Surrey in his first game at Lord's. Hendren welcomed him fulsomely before the game began and asked him what he did.

'I'm a fast bowler,' Gover replied.

'Well,' said Hendren, 'be careful how you bowl at me. I'm not as young as I used to be, and I don't like fast bowling so much.'

When Gover had his bowl at Hendren, there were three balls left in the over. The first was a bouncer and Hendren hooked it into the grandstand. He thought it must have been a fluke on Hendren's part so he tried another, which went for four. He put everything into the last ball of the over, another short one, which was again unceremoniously despatched for six in the same place as the first. As the fielders moved positions for the next over, Jack Hobbs passed Gover.

'Why are you bowling bouncers at Mr Hendren, son?' he asked.

'Because he doesn't like fast bowling,' came the answer.

Hobbs was astonished. 'Who on earth told you that?'

'He did, Mr Hobbs,' was the innocent reply.

'Then I am telling you,' Hobbs said with emphasis, 'that Pat is still as good a player of fast bowling as anyone I know. And what's more, young man, I'd remind you he's an Irishman and every night he kisses the Blarney Stone!'

Graeme Fowler:

In September 1985 I went to the Lancashire end-of-season party. I had been out of the first team for a few weeks because of a neck injury, so I didn't really fancy it at all – but it was great fun. Everyone was presented with a memento. I was given my second-team cap and an electric switch so that I could switch myself back on. Andy Hayhurst, known as 'Anus', got one of those big plastic tie-on bottoms that you strap round your waist – predictable but quite funny. David Hughes, who was moving into insurance as an outside interest, was given a bowler hat and a false nose – he has a large natural one.

Chris Maynard was given a dustbin lid with empty cans of lager tied round it – they reckoned he drank too much and they called him Grover after the character in *Sesame Street,* because he was always moaning and never had a good word to say about anybody. The hat was quite effective – it looked like an Australian hat, so he had it on all night.

Steve O'Shaughnessy was given a goldfish in a goldfish bowl. He was told, 'The reason we've given you this, Shauny, is we want you to watch it all winter. You'll see that no matter how many times it opens its mouth, nothing comes out.' John Stanworth then stuffed Shauny out of sight. He stuck his hand in the bag with the goldfish in the bowl, got this bit of carrot out, waggled it around and then ate it. Shauny went mad. 'You've eaten me fish! You've eaten me fish! The rotten git, he's eaten me fish!'

Of course everybody fell about. But then to cap it all, at the end of the evening just as everyone was leaving, Shauny was in the foyer carrying his fish and this drunken Scot rolled up to him, picked the fish out of the bowl and *did* eat it. This time Shauny thought, 'Oh, it's another bit of carrot, I'm not falling for that one again.' But in fact the Scotsman had quite calmly picked the fish out of the bowl, eaten it, and then cleared off as if nothing had happened.

Shauny was left with a bowl of water!

Brian Johnston:

One naughty story about Brian Close I think I can tell you. Close is ambidextrous, quite seriously – he plays golf left-handed or right-handed, equally well at either. Someone once said to him, 'How do you decide if you're going to play right-handed or left-handed?'

'Oh,' he said, 'it's quite easy. If I wake up and my wife's on her right side, I play right-handed and if she's on her left side, I play left-handed. It's as easy as that.'

So someone said, 'Yes, but what about if you wake up and she's lying on her back?'

'Oh,' he said, 'I ring up to say I'm going to be an hour late!'

Dickie Bird:

In a county match, Lancashire were playing Northamptonshire at Northampton. The match had finished and it was the last day. We were all coming off the field when Allan Lamb came up and shook hands with me. He said, 'Thanks for the game, Dickie. All the best. Have a good journey home.'

I said, 'Thank you, Lamby. See you later in the season.'

I had my shower, got changed, and went into the car park to get my car to drive home. I couldn't believe what I saw. He'd taken all four wheels off my car. It was jacked up. My wheels were at the side of the railings and he'd put a big notice on the windscreen: ALL THE BEST, DICKIE. HAVE A GOOD JOURNEY HOME!

Michael Parkinson:

When David Lloyd decided to play cricket for a living, the Wheel Tappers and Shunters Club lost a good comic. What cricket gained was a player able enough to captain his county, Lancashire, and almost captain his country.

He had an outside chance to be captain of England in 1980 when he was brought back for the one-day internationals against the West Indies. Lloyd's account of what happened is a perfect example of his droll style.

'I was told I'd be batting number seven and if I showed up well, got a few runs and handled the quicks okay, I would be in with a chance with a couple of others when it came to the captaincy. I remember taking guard and watching Malcolm Marshall walking back to his bowling mark. I thought to myself, "I don't go that far on my holidays."

'He set off towards me. He was halfway there when I thought, "I bet he doesn't want me to play forward to this delivery." He let go this ninety miles per hour thunderbolt at me and I played what I can only describe as a very hurried backward defensive prod. The ball smashed into my forearm and broke it in two places. As I was helped from the field, I remember thinking, "I wonder if I've done enough?"'

COUNTY CAPERS

Keith Fletcher:

It was in the early days of sponsorship, and Essex were due to play Middlesex the next day. We arrived at Lord's to find a large notice in the dressing room saying: 'NO TRACKSUITS ALLOWED ON THE PLAYING AREA'.

The Essex players, wearing our first sponsored tracksuits, had wandered down on to the hallowed turf to start fielding practice. Colonel John Stephenson, then secretary of MCC (a delightful man) saw us from his office window and announced over the Tannoy, 'No tracksuits to be worn on the playing area. Please remove your tracksuits.'

We all dutifully removed the offending apparel to reveal cricket whites – everyone, that is, except Ray East, who had nothing on *at all* under his tracksuit.

The Colonel, still on the Tannoy and in his best Oxford accent, said, 'Sensibly!'

Dickie Bird:

If you were to ask cricket lovers to nominate the most beautiful county ground many would go for Worcester, with good reason. You look through the trees to the cathedral and the River Severn, and when the flowers at New Road are in full bloom, it really is a marvellous sight.

Another feature at Worcester is the space reserved in the car park for the tea ladies. One anxious reporter, having arrived late at the ground for an important fixture, was looking for somewhere to park, when the attendant told him, 'Sorry, sir, I'm afraid you can't come in, there are no spaces left.'

'Yes, there are,' replied the reporter, pointing to several vacant spots.

'Oh,' said the attendant, 'but those are reserved for the tea ladies, sir.'

'But you surely don't need all that space for them,' complained the increasingly frustrated hack.

'Oh, but we do, sir,' replied the attendant. 'And I'll tell you this for nothing – it's a lot more important that we get our tea than you get anything in the paper, young man!'

Clive Radley:

A local derby – Middlesex v Surrey at Lord's. Pat Pocock (known throughout cricket as 'Percy') arrived at the crease to bat wearing spectacles, which nobody had seen him wearing before.

Fred Titmus, the bowler, politely enquired, 'What have you got those things on the end of your nose for, Perce?'

'They are because I'm bloody deaf. Why do you think?'

Titmus then bowled Pocock with his first delivery. As the dejected batsman walked past him back to the pavilion, Titmus remarked, 'You didn't hear that one too well, though, did you?'

Simon Hughes:

Durham's first Sunday League match of the 1993 season was against Lancashire at Old Trafford and our new polyester, coloured clothing gave us nipple rash. 'Lunch' between innings was not until 3.10 p.m. and I was famished midway through. I was out on the boundary and had to ask a spectator to buy me a packet of crisps.

When Mike Watkinson came in to bat, umpire Nigel Plews asked him what he wanted. Noting the official's bright blue coat, Watkinson said, 'Six gallons and a can of oil, please!'

Dickie Bird:

Yorkshire still play the odd game at Scarborough, a super ground, and their visits attract big gates. Scarborough is well known for the cricket festival, when various trophies are played for by Yorkshire and visiting guest teams. The cliffs overlooking the glorious North Bay are close at hand on one side of the ground, although not visible to the spectators, but there is a marvellous view of the North Yorkshire moors on the opposite side.

Bill Bowes, one of the best bowlers Yorkshire and England have ever had, covered cricket for the *Yorkshire Evening Post* when he retired from playing. He was faced with the usual problems of telephoning his reports from the ground to the sports desk back in Leeds, and during one Scarborough Festival week he sent the following item, 'After a quiet spell, Parfitt went down the wicket to Illingworth and edged him over the slips and into the deep for three.'

Unfortunately, the young lady on copy-taking duty that day had no interest whatsoever in cricket, and she typed out, 'After a quiet spell, Parfitt went down the wicket to Illingworth and edged him over the cliffs and into the deepest parts of the sea!'

Brian Johnston:

I am very much in favour of having a drink now and again because I think it is sociable but, in my job, you should never have too much. Of course, the same applies to cricket and I'll give you a good example. It concerns dear old 'Hopper' Levett. W.H.V. Levett was a great wicket-keeper and he kept wicket once for England against India, but mainly he used to keep for Kent when Les Ames or Godfrey Evans were playing for England. A very good wicket-keeper indeed, he stood up marvellously on the leg side. A great chap. He liked a glass of beer, and he smoked a foul-smelling pipe, but he was a lovely person.

One night, in 1947, he did have rather a heavy night and the next morning he had a most ghastly hangover. He went into the Kent dressing room and they helped him on with his socks and his boots, his pads, his box and his shirt. Kent were fielding, so they pushed him out on to the field, and a young fast bowler called Harding – who sadly died shortly after – had the ball.

So they put Levett down eighteen yards behind the stumps. He got down – he couldn't get any lower, his head was throbbing – and the first ball went *pheeww* past his right ear. He hadn't moved. Four byes. The next one went *pheeww* past his left ear. Four byes. That's eight byes in two balls and he hadn't moved.

The third ball, though, was outside the leg stump and the batsman reached forward and got an outside edge. The ball went very low on the leg side and old 'Hopper' took off and held a most brilliant catch, inches from the ground.

He threw the ball up in the air, went across to the slips and said, 'Do you know, gentlemen, I think that's the first time I've ever caught a batsman off the first ball of the day!'

Martin Johnson:

Leicestershire, so the match scorer alleges, beat Yorkshire by 9 runs at Scarborough on 31 August 1979 to win the Fenner Trophy. We'll have to take his word for it as close on seven thousand people barely witnessed a ball bowled in the most remarkable cricket match I've ever seen, or to be precise, never seen.

In the best 'show must go on' tradition, the big holiday crowd basked in a fog so thick it would have grounded every aircraft in the country. Only the occasional thwack of leather on willow convinced them that, somewhere in the vicinity, a cricket match was taking place – and this was in a year when the sponsors ordered the band to keep quiet during play to add a note of seriousness to the proceedings. I preferred the suggestion that they should strike up with, say, 'Colonel Bogey' when eone was out for a duck, or perhaps 'Slowboat to Australia' if Boycott had been batting. At least then we would have had a vague idea what was going on.

No soccer match would have started, but this game got under way just forty minutes late. It would have been thirty-five had the umpires not forgotten to bring out the ball. Leicestershire made a fine start thanks to Briers, who cracked six fours in his 36. I can only assume his breakfast consisted of carrot juice. Yorkshire opened with Old and Stevenson. For obvious reasons I can't tell you whether they performed well, although the bowling analyses indicate that Stevenson probably did not. Mind you, analyses might not be much to go by. During the later part of the innings the ball crossed the ropes in front of the press box with not a player in sight. The scorer took a guess and gave it to Clift off Stevenson, although it could just as easily have been to Birkenshaw off Oldham.

Dudleston's 14 in 21 overs suggested that he's happier batting when he can see the ball, but Davison and Balderstone put together a useful stand of 50 in only 11 overs before both fell in successive deliveries. Clift and Birkenshaw did even better, putting on 70 crucial runs in the last 11 overs. Birkenshaw's blade seemed to send the ball across the boundary every time it was wielded. But, once again, one could only get a vague impression of events. A tremendous cheer went up while these two were batting. Was it a six or was someone out? Then, as the mist lifted for a second or two, we noticed a beer lorry trundling through the main gates.

Leicestershire seemed destined to enjoy their ale more than their opponents would halfway through the Yorkshire innings when they stood at 79 for 3, still needing another 147. Shuttleworth then came on without anyone knowing it and removed Sharp, apparently lbw, and Sidebottom, appropriately enough, caught behind. Old, however, possesses a bat like a railway sleeper and, with sixes off Clift and Shuttleworth and a stand of 31 in three overs with Cope, he brought the target down from 46 off five overs to 10 off the last five balls. Higgs dropped short, Old hooked high and Briers took a well-judged catch to end it.

Simon Hughes:

On Sundays at Lord's during my benefit year at Middlesex in 1991, I took the unprecedented step of persuading flirtatious girlfriends in short skirts to go round with the buckets instead of the loyal old supporters who normally did it, and they regularly brought in £1,000 plus. The English currency – mostly coins but sometimes the odd fiver – was always augmented by francs, dollars, fruit-machine tokens and any other shrapnel people happened to have in their pockets.

It was the usual practice for the MCC to broadcast the proceeds over the Tannoy once they had been counted, and one Sunday I got them to announce: 'Simon Hughes thanks everyone who donated to today's benefit collection, which raised one thousand two hundred and thirty pounds thirty pence, seventy Canadian cents, fifty pesetas, one Kenyan shilling and two Iranian shekels.'

It got a better response than anything I'd ever achieved on the field, and all the collectors chuckled with self-satisfaction. We weren't quite so amused when the next morning we read that Bryan Robson's benefit match at Old Trafford had raised £340,000!

Richard Whiteley:

During the Scarborough Festival an avid young Yorkshire fan comes upon a stall at the local fairground announcing 'Marvo, the Miracle Memory Man'.

Intrigued, the fan enters the tent and finds, to his surprise, an American Indian lounging in a chair and drawing very slowly on his pipe.

'All right, mate?' says the Yorkshireman. The Indian removes the pipe from his mouth and with steely eyes says quietly, 'Where I come from, it is customary to greet a stranger with the word "How".'

Feeling a little intimidated, the fan responds, 'How, Marvo, what is this all about then?'

'I have a perfect and infallible memory,' says Marvo. 'Ask me anything.'

'I'll get this bugger,' says the fan to himself and asks, 'Who won the Gillette Cup final in 1965?'

'Yorkshire beat Surrey by 175 runs, 4 September 1965.'

'That's amazing,' says the Yorkshireman, and leaves shortly afterwards.

Some fifteen years later, the now-seasoned fan is back at the Festival and is most surprised to come upon 'Marvo, the Native American Memory Man' again.

'How,' he greets him.

Replies Marvo, 'Boycott 146, Illingworth 5 for 29.'

Fred Trueman:

The Yorkshire coach Arthur 'Ticker' Mitchell struck terror into the souls of a hundred youngsters; and undoubtedly he turned a similar number of raw schoolboys into county cricketers. Arthur was a man of dark intensity who always seemed to growl rather than speak. If the occasion arose when praise was called for, the words had to be forced reluctantly from a sparse vocabulary.

He might, of course, have had an entirely different personality at home, among his family, but somehow I doubt it. His son Alf was once chatting about the modern tendency to over-react to the taking of a wicket, by bowler and fieldsmen alike, with much embracing and exchanging of 'high fives'. Someone mischievously asked Alf how 'Ticker' would have viewed the spectacle of one cricketer kissing another.

'D'you know,' he replied thoughtfully, 'I can't even remember him kissing my mother!'

Dickie Bird:

Cedric Rhodes used to be the chairman of Lancashire County Cricket Club and one day he asked Farokh Engineer, in view of the continued hostilities between India and Pakistan, if there was any likelihood that he would be going home to fight for his country.

'Only if the fighting reaches my village,' said Farokh. 'Then, of course, I will have to go to protect my wife and children.'

Rhodes enquired, 'Which village is that?'

And Farokh replied, 'Altrincham!'

Brian Johnston:

Arthur Wood, the Yorkshire wicket-keeper, was in a match with a batsman who had played at and missed three successive balls, each of which just grazed the stumps without disturbing the bails. Arthur asked him, 'Have you ever tried walking on water?'

On another occasion Yorkshire were playing the South Africans at Bramall Lane in 1935 and H.B. Cameron went in to face the bowling of Hedley Verity. Cameron took guard and hit the first ball over the pavilion for six. The next three balls all went for four and the last two for six each, making 30 runs off the over.

When Verity passed Arthur Wood at the end of the over, his face was as long as a collie's.

'Don't you worry, Hedley,' said Wood, 'you've got him in two minds.'

'Two minds?' said Verity. 'What do you mean, two minds?'

'Oh,' said Wood, 'he doesn't know whether to hit you for four or six!'

Fred Trueman:

A man with a personality all his own was Emmott Robinson, who did not play first-class cricket until he was in his mid-thirties, which is probably why he quickly assumed a sense of seniority. Emmott was what would today be called a 'bowling all-rounder'.

I suppose the Roses matches in the earlier half of the twentieth century might have been designed with Emmott Robinson in mind. It is said that he was the first to arrive on one occasion, so he knelt down in the dressing room and offered up a prayer, which went something along these lines:

'Oh Almighty God, thou alone can decide what the weather will be like for this match. If it is fine and Lancashire play better they will win. And if Yorkshire play better, *they* will win. But, oh dear Lord, if tha will just keep out on it for t'next three days, we'll knock bloody 'ell out on 'em!'

Simon Hughes:

I discovered a whole new vocabulary during my opening season in first-class cricket in 1980. Here's a list of the jargon I learned:

Aerosol bowler Someone, usually a paceman, who 'sprays it everywhere'.

Bunsen (burner) Turning pitch. Raging bunsens are often found in India.

Cafeteria bowling A load of dross, so the batsman can 'help himself'.

Cardboard cut-outs Immobile slip fielders.

Crusted Batsman hit on head by a bouncer.

Dinkies Second team.

Dollies Stumps.

Donks Outfielders, usually lumbering fast bowlers.

Filth Bowling that promotes a flier.

Flier Rapid run-scoring at the start of an innings.

German general Batting side encouraging the ball to boundary (after Goebbels).

Gnat Seam bowler of negligible pace.

Grabbers Slip fielders.

Headless chicken Bowler who tears in wildly with a crazed expression.

Jaffa Unplayable delivery.

Jugged, going for the jug Bowler savaged by a rampant batsman.

Knacker Ball, delivery.

Lenny Batsman who favours leg-side shots.

Nick Faint edge, or another word for 'form'.

On 'em Batsman arriving for the second innings having got nought in the first.

Pongo Rapid scoring.

Rabbit Hopeless tailender.

Sawn off Dodgy umpiring decision.

Spitting cobra Delivery that rears abruptly from a length.

Strangle Wicket with rotten delivery. The bowler is often labelled 'Boston'.

Trolleyed Player (usually the captain) losing his temper.

Up the ladder Injured player suspected of hypochondria.

Xs Captain's allowance for a round of drinks after a day's play.

Fred Trueman:

George Hirst was a magnificent player for Yorkshire and England in the early part of the twentieth century and he later became an excellent coach. In one remarkable season George scored 2,385 runs and took 208 wickets. When asked if he thought anyone would ever beat it, he replied, 'I don't know, but if he does he'll be bloody tired!'

Brian Johnston:

In a Lancashire match a fast bowler was bowling on a bad wicket, and the opening batsman had to face a number of terrifying deliveries. The first whizzed past his left ear, the second nearly knocked his cap off, and the third struck him an awful blow over the heart. He collapsed and lay on the ground – then, after a minute or two, he got up and prepared to take strike again. The umpire asked him if he was ready and he replied, 'Yes, but I would like the sightscreen moved.'

'Certainly,' said the umpire. 'Where would you like it?'

The batsman replied, 'About halfway down the wicket between me and the bowler!'

Dickie Bird:

A Yorkshireman who played with Northamptonshire in the 1950s was Des Barrick, a big practical joker, who was born in the same row of terraced houses as Geoff Boycott.

The legendary fast bowler Frank Tyson was one of Des's team-mates. Now Frank did not care much for the ground at Derby, but there was one consolation – the enormous antique baths, ideal for a post-match soak when the old bones were aching like mad and the biting wind had reached the parts that other winds could not reach. One typically freezing day, he had jumped straight in the huge bath and was just beginning to get some feeling back into his fingers and toes when Des 'Roly-Poly' Barrick tiptoed in and poured a bucket of ice-cold water over him.

Frank almost hit the ceiling, not to mention Des. In any case, the cackling Des was off like a shot. So Frank decided on revenge. He wrapped his towel round him, filled another bucket with ice-cold water, marched into the adjoining room where Des was sitting, and poured it over his colleague's head.

Des was fully dressed by this time, and he stood there, as if in a state of shock, with the water soaking into his clothes. A wicked grin slowly spread across his face and Frank was a bit taken aback. Then came the punchline. Chortled Des, 'I've got news for thee, Frank, old lad. I rather thought you might try summat like that, so I've put *thy* clothes on!'

Martin Johnson:

Back in 1986, when an opposition batsman sent up a skier at Grace Road, Leicester and the cry from the fielders went up, 'Yours, Ted!' it may not have been immediately apparent to spectators exactly who had been elected to take the catch. They should have kept their eyes on Tim Boon. He, to all in the dressing room, was the aforementioned 'Ted'. He bore no resemblance to a former Conservative Prime Minister, didn't need a fluffy toy to soothe himself to sleep, and was too young to have gone through his teens wearing winkle-pickers, hair slicked back with Brylcreem. So why Ted?

It dated back to a civic reception in Bristol two years earlier, when the players, all togged up, were being introduced by one of those uniformed commissionaires with a booming toastmaster's voice. 'Name, please,' he inquired. 'Tim Boon,' came the whispered reply. 'Ladies and gentlemen, I present . . . Mr Ted Moon!' Collapse of assembled cricketers. The name stuck, and Boon was instantly lifted out of the category in which 90 per cent of cricketers find themselves when the nicknames are handed out – just add a 'y'. 'Boony, Cobby, Steeley, Baldy, Benjy, Potsy, Aggy . . .'

Nicknames are compulsory for county cricketers. It must be something to do with the boarding-school syndrome, where everyone is away from home and lumped together. For prep school read dressing room, for dormitory read hotel bedroom. When Laurie Potter arrived at Grace Road, David Gower temporarily gave up on the *Telegraph* crossword, and pondered about the new man. 'How about "Lobster"?' Lobster, Potter, get it? Anyway, it didn't stick.

Most nicknames are boring, others unable to be reproduced in a family publication. Some are quite good. Romaines was 'Human', Aworth 'Rita', Derrick 'Bo', Weston 'Spaghetti', Bakker 'Nip', and dear old Graham Parsons, not noted for shrewdness or clarity of vision when the heat was on out in the middle, was 'Cement-head'.

David Steele picked up one of the better ones. His fondness for being last in the queue when the rounds were being bought remains legendary, and so he became 'Crime' – doesn't pay!

DOWN UNDER

Darren Gough:

On my first tour of Australia in 1994/95 England took part in a one-day tournament with Australia, an Australian 'A' team and Zimbabwe. After losing our opener against Australia, we went down twice in a single weekend to the Australian Cricket Academy – fortunately, I had a slight hamstring strain – and then to Zimbabwe in Sydney. I didn't play at Toowoomba, where Mike Gatting hit a double hundred before being hit in the mouth while fielding.

Our physio ordered him not to eat that night, but we spotted a couple of empty pizza boxes outside his room. Gatt claimed he'd been framed. That was rich. I remember asking him directions in Sydney. He replied, 'Easy. It's right at the Italian, left at the curry house and just beyond the Chinese!'

Brian Johnston:

On the 1924/25 MCC tour of Australia, Andrew Sandham, the Surrey and England opening batsman, was fielding on the boundary near the famous Hill at the Sydney Cricket Ground. Someone in the crowd kept shouting, 'Sandy, ask your skipper to send out someone else, you're too ugly!'

After this had been going on for some time Sandham got fed up with it and told his captain, Arthur Gilligan, who suggested that he send Patsy Hendren to field out there. Hendren made his way towards the Hill and had got only halfway there when another shout went up, 'Send back Sandham!'

Michael Parkinson:

Jack Fingleton once told me about the time he first opened for New South Wales with the legendary Charlie Macartney. 'As he walked to the wicket, Macartney said to me, "Now think on, young Fingleton, be ready first ball." I would have done anything for him but I wasn't sure what he meant. Did he mean be prepared for a quick single? Was he telling me to concentrate from the first moment?

'All these questions were racing through my mind as

the fast bowler raced in for the first ball and as he did I saw Macartney walking down the wicket with his bat at shoulder level.

'In an instant several things happened. The bowler bowled and Macartney, halfway down the wicket, gave it an awesome smack. The bowler dived for cover, so did I. The ball hit the sightscreen on the full and bounced back fifty yards on to the field of play.

'It was the most audacious shot I have ever seen. As I lay there alongside the fast bowler, who was by now a gibbering wreck, I saw the batsman standing above me tapping the wicket with his bat. "Just like I said, young Fingleton. Always ready from the first ball." He looked at the hapless bowler and said confidentially, "They don't like it, you know!"'

Fred Trueman:

The Australians have what might be described as a more cynical approach to umpiring – at least that was my experience on the 1958/59 tour when our batsmen were given no protection at all against the 'suspect' deliveries of Ian Meckiff, Gordon Rorke and Keith Slater. I vividly remember one conversation in which one of us drew attention to Slater's action and an Aussie official grinned, 'Well, at least he's chucking *straight*, isn't he, mate?'

Brian Johnston:

A batsman in a match at the Sydney Cricket Ground had played and missed a number of times. Finally, Yabba, the famous Sydney Hill barracker, shouted out to the bowler, 'Send him down a grand piano, and see if he can play *that*!'

Darren Gough:

At the end of the fourth day in the Boxing Day Test at Melbourne in 1994, England were on 79 for 4 and Alec Stewart was coming in at number seven because of a broken finger. The fifth day's play lasted 12.3 overs and produced just 13 runs, as well as a little piece of cricket history. Shane Warne, wicketless up to that point in our second innings, took the first Ashes hat-trick for over ninety years. Phil DeFreitas was the first, lbw playing back. Off I set. At 91 for 7, I'm not sure what my game-plan was. It didn't matter. Warnie got one to turn and bounce. I tried to leave it but Ian Healy took a great catch as it flew off my glove. As I turned to leave, I suddenly realised what a big ground the MCG is and what a long way back it was. The stupid duck was quacking on the big screen and the crowd was roaring, 'Warnie, Warnie,' at the prospect of their favourite son taking a Test hat-trick on his home ground.

I suppose there is no better sight for a bowler on a hat-trick than seeing Devon Malcolm walk out. In golfing terms, it's the nearest thing you can get to a 'gimme'. As Devon passed me, 'Good luck' was all I could think of to say. He was still fiddling with his thigh pad and gloves. We all knew what was coming – the googly, it had to be. The expected Devon wind-up never came. He pushed forward, the ball hit his glove and David Boon took a magnificent catch at short square. The MCG went wild.

'Why didn't you have a go at him, Dev?'

His reply was pure Devon. 'I was going to, but then I thought I'd play properly.'

Properly! Can you believe it? Shane Warne on a hat-trick and Devon Malcolm thinks he can bat!

Michael Parkinson:

Keith Miller had the capacity to talk a leg off an iron pot when the mood took him and I would just listen. He told me this story about Arthur Morris:

'I once bowled him eight bouncers in an over. There had been a lot of discussion in the press about short-pitched bowling. There was a lot of talk about banning it or limiting the number of bouncers so I thought I'd have a spot of fun.

'When Arthur came out to bat I put nine men on the

square-leg boundary and just bowled at his head. When I bowled the first one Arthur said, "Oh dear, a bouncer." And every time I bowled another, he'd say, "Oh my God, he's done it again." And it so tickled me that I started laughing so much that the tears were running down my face as I came in to bowl. I could hardly make it to the crease. Old Arthur was in a right state.'

'Was Morris all right?' I inquired.

'All right?' said Miller. 'He hit me for thirty-four in the over!'

Brian Johnston:

Godfrey Evans, the Kent and England wicket-keeper, made a particularly good stumping on the leg side when playing in an up-country match on one of his tours of Australia. As he whipped off the bails he shouted to the umpire, 'How's that?'

The umpire replied, 'Bloody marvellous!'

Ian Brayshaw:

A balmy afternoon during a Test match at the Melbourne Cricket Ground was rudely interrupted by a between-overs announcement through the public address system.

'Would Mr J. Smith of Hawthorn please go home,'

the voice announced. 'Your wife is having her baby and must be taken to hospital.'

Laughter flowed around the ground as the spectators pictured a harassed father-to-be hurrying off home to his wife. Not so, however, because after about half an hour the voice again boomed across the ground, this time with some urgency:

'Repeating our earlier message to Mr J. Smith of Hawthorn . . . would he please go home immediately, because his wife is in labour and must be taken to hospital straight away.'

Much more mirth from the crowd, this time picturing a man reluctant to leave the cricket – but surely by now bidding farewell to his mates to dash to his vehicle and tear off home. How wrong were twenty thousand spectators! Much to their delight, the now pleading message was repeated with grim urgency some twenty minutes later. After a further thirty minutes had passed there was a bland announcement:

'Would Mr J. Smith of Hawthorn please go to the Mercy Hospital, where his wife has now given birth to a baby son!'

Brian Johnston:

While he was in Australia with the 1962/63 MCC team, the Reverend David Sheppard came in for more than his fair share of dropped catches. The story was going around that a young English couple, who had settled in Australia, were due to have their first-born christened. The husband suggested that it would be nice if they got David Sheppard to do it for them.

'Oh no,' said the horrified wife, 'not likely, he would only drop it!'

Fred Trueman:

On the 1958/59 MCC tour of Australia I learned a lot about cricket, but also about how Australians view themselves:

The bigger the hat, the smaller the sheep farm.
The shorter the nickname, the more they warm to you.
Whether it is the opening of Parliament in Canberra or a new fine art gallery in Sydney, there is no formal event in Australia that can't be improved by a sausage sizzle.
They will refer to their best friend as 'a total bastard', whereas their worst enemy is 'a bit of a bastard'.
When invited to a party, the done thing is to take along

a bottle of cheap red wine that slides down the throat like a rusty knife, then spend the evening drinking the host's tinnies. One should never feel self-conscious about doing that, as the host will expect it from you and will have catered for it.

When out in the territories, the neon sign advertising the motel's pool will be slightly larger than the pool itself.

The true mark of the esteem in which an Australian cricketer is held is not having a stand named after him, but a bar in the ground – better still, a urinal, as in 'The Wally Grout Gents' in Sydney.

The benchmark of a man's masculinity is to erect a beach umbrella in the face of a strong south-easterly.

The wise person chooses a partner who is not only attractive to them, but also to midges and mosquitoes.

Barry Johnston:

In December 2004 a vital league match between the Inverloch Cricket Club and their local rivals Nerrena in Victoria, Australia, ended in chaos after the visitors were served green-speckled cupcakes during the tea interval. The Nerrena players claimed later that the cakes were laced with marijuana, although the Inverloch club secretary dismissed the allegations as simply 'rumours'.

Nerrena player Tim Clark recalled, 'I thought, gee, this is pretty good, they usually feed us crap.' In fact the cupcakes were so delicious that Clark ate five and two of his team-mates polished off the remainder. Things started to fall apart for the Nerrena side after tea when one player took nearly twenty minutes to put on his pads. The two others kept breaking into hysterical laughter and had to dash off the field during play for drinks of water. Not surprisingly, this extraordinary behaviour unnerved the rest of the team and Nerrena lost by 50 runs. The two Victorian sides were in a relegation battle at the bottom of their local league and Nerrena were consigned to the second division.

After the match, Tim Clark still felt rather light-headed but he had to assemble a kit bike for a fundraiser that evening. Clark confessed, 'After a small lie-down I tried to follow the instructions but I was all over the shop. I was putting the handlebars where the seat was meant to be!' When he finally completed the bike he was four hours late for the club function.

Somehow the three Nerrena players who had scoffed all the cakes managed to drive themselves home but they had a lucky escape. As one admitted later, if the police had tested him for drugs on the way home and he had come up positive, what could he have told them? 'Sorry, officer. It wasn't me. I was fed drugged cupcakes at the cricket!'

Brian Johnston:

There's a lovely cricket story about the late Duke of
Norfolk, who went as the manager of Ted Dexter's team
to Australia in 1962/63. They loved him in Australia –
they called him 'Dukey' – because wherever MCC played
he leased a racehorse and ran it in the local meeting.

MCC were playing against South Australia at
Adelaide, and about twenty-two miles outside Adelaide
there is a racecourse called Gawlor. There's a lovely
paddock there with eucalyptus trees and gum trees, very
picturesque.

The Duke had a horse running there, so he thought
he would go and see it. He spotted it under the eucalyptus
tree and walked across the paddock in his pinstriped
suit, panama hat and MCC ribbon, very much the Duke.
As he approached, to his horror, he saw the trainer put
his hand in his pocket and give the horse something to
eat.

He thought, 'Oh, my God, I'm a member of the Jockey
Club at home,' and he went up to the trainer and said,
'I hope you didn't give him anything you shouldn't have,
trainer. We don't want any trouble with dope here.'

'No, no, Your Grace,' said the trainer. 'I just gave him
a lump of sugar. I'm going to eat one myself. Would
you like one too, Your Grace?'

The Duke thought he'd better humour him, so he ate

the lump of sugar, talked about the race and went off to watch it from the grandstand. Five minutes before the race started, in came the jockeys, waddling as they do.

The Duke's jockey went up under the eucalyptus tree to his horse and the trainer said, 'Look. This is a seven-furlong race. The first five furlongs, keep tucked in behind and don't move. But for the last two furlongs, give him all you've got, and if anyone passes you after that, it's either the Duke of Norfolk or myself!'

Fred Trueman:

The Reverend David Sheppard had one or two catching lapses on the 1962/63 MCC tour of Australia. They were all the more poignant to me because they occurred when he was fielding at short fine-leg, a position I regarded very definitely as mine. I couldn't field there to my own bowling, of course, and so the future Bishop of Liverpool was occasionally to be found there. Eventually, his mistakes caused him to be moved to *deep* fine-leg, and it was there that his moment of triumph came . . . or so he thought. Fred Titmus dropped one short, the batsman hooked, and Sheppard, on the boundary, held the catch.

In a frenzy of delight, he hurled the ball high into the air and, as he waited for the ball to return to his hands, the voice of Brian Statham was heard from the neighbouring third man: 'You'd better chuck it in, Rev. It was a no-ball and they're on their third run!'

Brian Johnston:

Whenever I go out to Australia I always fly straight back, I don't stop off for a day's rest on the way. But when I was there last time we had a married couple with us and they decided to have three days in Bangkok on the way back. They had two very pleasant days and on the last day the wife said, 'I'm going shopping, you go and amuse yourself.'

He thought, 'Good idea!' So he went to the hotel porter and got the address of a massage parlour. He went and knocked on the door and a little Thai girl came and said, 'What can I do for you, sir?'

He said, 'I'd like a massage.'

'Certainly, sir.'

'How much will that be?'

'A thousand dollars.'

'Oh,' he said, 'I can't afford a thousand dollars. Two hundred dollars is the most that I can afford.'

She said, 'I'm sorry, a thousand is our price. You'd better go somewhere else.'

Well, he didn't bother. He went window shopping and went to pick up his wife at the appointed time. They were walking back to the hotel when down the street came this Thai girl, who looked at his wife and said, 'There you are. See what you get for two hundred dollars!'

Ian Botham:

I have many great memories of touring with the England team during my cricket career, and numerous stories to tell about my room-mates! However, one man stands out in particular – Derek Randall, or 'Arkle' as he is known to his fellow players and friends.

On returning to his hotel room in Adelaide, following a day in the field, he decided to run a bath. Having turned the water on, he remembered that he needed to pass on a message to Messrs I.T. Botham and A.J. Lamb. He quickly wrapped a towel around his body and slipped across the corridor to our room. We opened the door to Arkle, invited him in for a drink (a cup of Earl Grey, of course) and spent a while chatting. On leaving, he realised that he had left his key inside his own room. Unlike most people, instead of asking either Lamby or myself to ring down to reception, he decided to go down himself.

At the Adelaide Hilton that night, there was a rather special function, with people from all over Australia arriving dressed in DJs – the works. As the towel-clad Arkle arrived at the reception desk, there was utter chaos, with people running hell for leather out of the dining room, some soaking wet.

While asking the very flustered receptionist if he could have another key for his room, he also inquired what the problem was.

'Some stupid **** has left their bath water running and flooded the dining area!'

No need to ask who, as she handed over the replacement key to a slightly under-dressed Mr Randall!

Brian Johnston:

It was a Sunday during the MCC tour of Australia in 1928/29. Patsy Hendren and Percy Chapman, the England captain, decided to get away from it all and they borrowed a car for a run into the country. After a few miles they went round a corner and saw a cricket match about to start in a field adjoining the road. As all cricketers are wont to do, they stopped the car with the intention of watching the game for a few minutes. The car had no sooner stopped than an Australian strolled over and said, 'Do either of you chaps play cricket?'

Chapman pointed to Hendren and said, 'He plays a little.'

'Good oh,' said the fellow, 'we are a man short. Will you make up for us?'

Although it was Patsy's day off he obliged, and as his adopted side were fielding the captain sent him out to long-on. Patsy went to the allotted position, and as the field was on a slope he was out of sight of the pitch. He had nothing to do except throw the ball in occasionally. He was lost to sight for a long time when at last a towering hit was sent in his direction. Patsy caught the ball and ran up the hill shouting, 'I caught it, I caught it.'

The batsman looked at him with daggers drawn – it was *his* captain. 'You lunatic . . . they were out twenty minutes ago. *We* are batting now!'

Ian Brayshaw:

The Indian cricket team made a most disappointing start to its three-Test series in Australia in 1980/81. The tourists went down by an innings in the First Test, which began in Sydney just after Christmas. The margin was largely due to a fighting double century by Australian Greg Chappell, but aided by some most irresponsible strokeplay by the Indians.

After the game, the Indian captain Sunil Gavaskar was asked for his comments on the ignominious defeat. The little fellow forced a smile and said, 'We gave away our wickets like Christmas presents . . . trouble is, we Indians don't celebrate Christmas!'

The Third Test in that Indian series was played at the Melbourne Cricket Ground and one prominently displayed sign summed up the tourists' batting woes: 'You Indians eat a lot of curry . . . why don't you get the runs?'

Barry Johnston:

In 1971 anti-apartheid protestors disrupted a South African rugby union tour of Australia. There were several angry disturbances and the Australian Cricket Board decided at the last minute to cancel a tour by South Africa planned for later that year. Instead, they invited a Rest of the World XI, under the captaincy of Garry Sobers, to play a five Test series against Australia.

Before the First Test in Brisbane, the members of the Rest of the World team were met at the airport by a group of Australian officials. One of the Rest of the World players was the young South-African-born Tony Greig, who would make his England debut the following year. Greig was introduced to an elderly gentleman by his team-mate and fellow countryman Hilton Ackerman, who then left them alone. Greig didn't quite get the old man's name and spent a few minutes making small talk. Then he asked the elderly gentleman to hold his bag while he went to the toilet.

When Greig returned, he sat down and, since the other

man was very quiet, he tried to make some polite conver-sation with him. He asked him if he was with the Australian Board and the elderly gentleman replied yes, he was. Then Greig asked him if he had himself played any cricket in his life, to which the elderly gentleman also answered, 'Yes.'

Still none the wiser, Greig said, 'I'm sorry, but I didn't get your name.'

The elderly gentleman replied, 'Donald Bradman.'

Brian Johnston:

A lovely story is told about Brian Close. He was the youngest person ever to represent England – eighteen in 1949 – and then he went out to Australia with Freddie Brown as the junior member of the side in 1950/51. He made a hundred in the first match and hardly any runs after that – not a great tour for him.

They were going up by train from Sydney to Newcastle, as they did in those days; it was in the evening and there was a girl sitting in the carriage, nursing a baby. The chap opposite her kept looking at the baby and she said, 'What are you looking at my baby for?'

'I'd rather not say.'

'What are you looking for?' she went on, and in the end he said, 'All right, I'll tell you. It's the ugliest looking baby I've ever seen in my life!'

Well, she rose and burst into tears. She was standing out in the corridor, weeping her eyes out and holding her baby, when the MCC team came along on the way to supper. Bringing up the rear was the junior man, Brian Close, who saw this girl and said, 'What's wrong, dear. Can I help?'

'Yes. I've been insulted by that man in the carriage,' she said and burst into tears again.

'I'll tell you what,' Brian said. 'Before I have supper, I'll go along to the restaurant car and bring you back a cup of tea to cheer you up.'

She said, 'Oh, please,' and burst into tears again.

He came back two minutes later and she was still crying. 'There you are, dear,' he said, 'a cup of tea to cheer you up. And what's more, I've also brought a banana for the monkey!'

GAFFES AND GIGGLES

Brian Johnston:

One serious bit of advice. Nothing to do with cricket really, but if you're making a speech at a cricket dinner, or anywhere, and you make a mistake, never stop to apologise, because if you do, people know you've made a mistake. If you don't apologise and go straight on, people say, 'What did he say?' and, by that time, you're talking about something else.

I've carried this out over my cricket career, because I'm famous for making quite a lot of gaffes. I don't do them on purpose, but in a six-hour day you're bound to make the odd mistake. A lot of them are very old, but here are one or two:

In 1961 at Headingley, the Australians were fielding and I was doing the television. The camera panned in and showed Neil Harvey at leg-slip, and he filled the screen. Now if you're doing a television commentary and someone fills the screen, you've got to be very quick to talk about him, otherwise the camera goes off and shows something else and you've missed the chance.

So without thinking, very hurriedly, I said, 'There's Neil Harvey standing at leg-slip, with his legs wide apart waiting for a tickle!'

I realised immediately what I'd said and wished the earth would open and swallow me up. The Australian commentator Jack Fingleton made matters worse by drawing attention to it, saying, 'I beg your pardon. I presume you mean waiting for a catch.'

I didn't speak for about three minutes after that!

Then I went to Hove, for radio, where Sussex were playing Hampshire. Hampshire had a chap called Henry Horton who had a funny stance. When he batted, he stood more or less parallel to the ground, leaned right forward and stuck his bottom out.

I thought I ought to let the listeners know, so I said, 'He's got a funny stance, he sticks his bottom out.'

Then I meant to say, 'He looks like he's *sitting* on a *shooting* stick,' but I got it the wrong way round!

When Ray Illingworth was captaining Leicestershire, the studio came over to me and I said, 'Welcome to Leicester, where Ray Illingworth has just relieved himself at the Pavilion End!'

At Worcester I once greeted the listeners with, 'Welcome to Worcester, where you've just missed seeing Barry Richards hitting one of Basil D'Oliveira's balls clean out of the ground!'

At Old Trafford on a Saturday – England against India – it was a dreadful day, pelting with rain and very cold. All the Indian spectators were huddled together in the crowd, looking miserable. Radio Three came over to me, asking, 'Any chance of any play today, Brian?'

I said, 'No, it's wet, it's cold and it's miserable.' I meant to say, 'There's a dirty black cloud,' instead of which I said, 'There's a dirty black *crowd*,' and there they all were!

Henry Blofeld:

Ollie Milburn was used on several occasions as a summariser on *Test Match Special* and he made some telling contributions. He will probably be remembered longest, however, for an unfortunate gaffe during a Test at Headingley. He was asked to be in the commentary box at about eight o'clock one morning to do the early breakfast-time programmes.

When the time came, they were unable to raise him at the ground and so they checked at the hotel. Sure enough, Milburn had overslept, but he was told that it would be fine and he could do the programme on the telephone from his room, making it sound as if he was at the ground. The interview started promisingly. Then, halfway through, the interviewer suddenly asked him what the weather was like.

'I don't know,' came the reply. 'I haven't opened the curtains yet!'

Brian Johnston:

John Snagge was a marvellous chap. He was the voice of Great Britain. Every big occasion – the Allied landings, Winston Churchill's death, the King's death – he was always the voice they put on the air and he represented us all.

He was a tremendous announcer in that way but he didn't normally do the sports news. One day he was asked to read it and he got as far as the cricket scores, when he said, 'Yorkshire two hundred and fifty-nine all out. Hutton ill . . . Oh, I'm sorry, Hutton one hundred and eleven!'

Dickie Bird:

My most embarrassing moment as an umpire was when nature called and I came off the field at Old Trafford and stopped a Test match. Ian Botham was bowling from my end and I said, 'I've got to go off, Both, I've got to go to the toilet.'

He said, 'You can't, we're in the middle of a Test match. There's still an hour left to go before lunch.'

I said, 'I've got to go,' and he said, 'Well, if you gotta go, you gotta go!'

So I said, 'I'm sorry, gentlemen, but nature calls.'

I just ran off the field, went into the toilet, and came back down the members' enclosure at Old Trafford. It was a full house and as I came out, I was pulling up my zip . . . and the crowd erupted!

Brian Johnston:

I was at Southampton one Saturday to commentate on a match between Hampshire and Surrey. Rex Alston was up at Edgbaston covering one of Warwickshire's matches and close of play there was not until 7 p.m.

At 6.30 p.m. at Southampton, as the players left the field, I said something like, 'Well, that's close of play here with Hampshire three hundred and one all out. But they go on playing till seven o'clock at Edgbaston, so over there now for some more balls from Rex Alston!'

Rex himself is reputed to have said, 'Over now to Old John Arlott at Trafford!' He also once reported that a captain had asked for 'the medium pace roller!'

Then at Lord's during a Middlesex match, Rex

surprised many listeners when he announced, 'No runs from that over bowled by Jack Young, which means that he has now had four maidens on the trot!'

Henry Blofeld:

Johnners used to ring me up and tell me silly stories. The telephone went one morning and he said, 'Do you know the one about the jump leads?'

I said, 'No.'

He said, 'There was this chap who got an invitation to a fancy-dress ball at the Dorchester and it said: P.S. Bring the invitation with you. He went but he went naked. He had nothing but jump leads all over him. He arrived at the door and the chap said, "You can't come in here like that."

'He said, "I've come to the party, here's my invitation."

'"But it's a fancy-dress party. You can't possibly come in like that."

'He said, "I've *come* in fancy dress."

'"What on earth have you come as?"

'He said, "Any fool, anyone with the meanest intellect, can see what I've come as . . . I've come as a jump lead."

'The chap rather grudgingly said, "Well, yes, I suppose you have," and he stood aside and let him go through. As he went in, the doorman shouted after him, "But don't you start anything!"'

Brian Johnston:

During the Third Test match of England's tour of the Caribbean in 1960, the West Indian commentator Roy Lawrence welcomed listeners by saying, 'It's another wonderful day here at Sabina Park . . . the wind shining and the sun blowing gently across the field!'

On England's tour of Australia in 1978/79, another commentator said, 'John Emburey is bowling with three short-legs – one of them wearing a helmet!'

And an unknown commentator is reported to have informed his radio audience, 'He was bowled by a ball which he should have left alone!'

Barry Johnston:

Brian was renowned for his practical jokes in the box but his fellow commentators would occasionally get their own back. The stakes seem to have been raised when Jonathan Agnew joined the team as the new BBC Cricket Correspondent in 1991. The two of them usually broadcast at different times, which meant that any practical jokes required advance planning.

Neville Oliver was the popular Australian commentator, promptly renamed 'Dr NO' as soon as Brian saw his initials listed on the commentators' rota. During the 1993 Ashes series, Agnew recruited the Doctor to help him pull off a classic practical joke. They had received a list of the people who would be making the presentations on the pavilion balcony after the match. Agnew talked his idea over with the Doctor and then surreptitiously typed an additional name at the bottom of the list, photocopying the page to make it look more realistic.

Before the presentation ceremony he handed the paper over to Brian, who proceeded to read the list out on the air, including the surprise announcement that also present on the balcony was the managing director of the Cornhill Insurance Group, Mr Hugh Jarce!

Brian Johnston:

One of the great things for me is the number of letters we get from young boys and girls, which is good, because I know how difficult it is for cricket in schools nowadays.

Sometimes the letters are technical. They want to know about laws, or about cricketers, and we had a wonderful one a few years ago.

Fred had been going on all afternoon, saying, 'Johnners, cricket is a sideways game. Get the left shoulder over the elbow, a straight bat – sideways on. When you're bowling – sideways – get the swivel action, look over your left shoulder. It's a sideways game, Johnners, a sideways game.'

He went on like this and he was quite right. It *is* a sideways game. About four days later, we got a letter from a young boy, who wrote: 'Dear Mr Trueman, I was listening to you the other day about cricket being a sideways game. I'm afraid it hasn't worked with me. I'm a wicket-keeper and I let eighteen byes in the first over!'

The other thing they do is send me stupid riddles: 'Ask Fred what animal he would like to be if he was standing naked in a snow storm.'

'I don't know, Johnners. What animal would I like to be?'

'The answer is: a little 'otter!'

They send terrible jokes: 'What's a Frenchman called if he's shot out of a cannon?'

'I don't know, Johnners.'

'Napoleon Blownapart!'

'Who was the ice-cream man in the Bible?'

'No idea.'

'Walls of Jericho!'

Someone rang in and said, 'What about Lyons of Judah?'

And one day a young boy came up to me at Trent Bridge and said, 'Mr Johnston, did you hear about the man who went to the doctor?'

I said, 'No.'

'Oh,' he said, 'he told the doctor that he wasn't feeling

at all well. He said that in the morning he thinks he's a wigwam and in the afternoon he's a marquee. So the doctor looked at him and said, "All right, I'll give you a sedative. You're obviously *two tents*!"'

Ian Brayshaw:

Even the legendary Australian radio commentator Alan McGilvray occasionally did not say things quite how he might have meant them to be. Like the time in the heart of the 1980/81 season when he summed up a batting failure by Kim Hughes:

'Well, it has been a weekend of delight and disappointment for Kim Hughes – his wife presented him with twins yesterday . . . and a "duck" today!'

Brian Johnston:

My most unfortunate gaffe was in 1969 at Lord's where Alan Ward of Derbyshire was playing in his very first Test match, bowling very fast from the Pavilion End to Glenn Turner of New Zealand.

Off the fifth ball of one of his overs, he got Glenn Turner a terrible blow in the box. Turner collapsed, his bat going one way, his gloves another. The cameras panned in and I had to waffle away, pretending he had been hit anywhere but where he had – as it was a bit rude!

After about three minutes he got up, someone gave him his bat, and I said, 'He looks very pale. Very plucky of him, he's going on batting. One *ball* left!'

Then there was the one that I didn't know I'd said. I'm still not sure whether I did or not! That was after the 1976 match against the West Indies at The Oval, when I received a letter from a lady called Miss Mainpiece, who wrote: 'Dear Mr Johnston, we do enjoy your commentaries, but you must be more careful, as we have a lot of young people listening. Do you realise what you said the other day? They came over to you as Michael Holding was bowling to Peter Willey and you said, "Welcome to The Oval where the bowler's Holding, the batsman's Willey!"'

On another occasion I was doing a commentary on the annual Whitsun match at Lord's. Middlesex always used to play Sussex, and Middlesex were batting, captained by John Warr. They had made about 300 for 3 by tea and I handed back to the studio for the tea interval. They came back to me after tea with, 'Over now to Brian Johnston for the latest news at Lord's.'

'Well,' I said, 'the latest news at Lord's is that Warr's declared.' And, you've got to believe it, the BBC duty officer said an old lady rang up to see who it was against!

Barry Johnston:

As he approached eighty years old, Brian found it harder to control his laughter. The slightest hint of anything *risqué* would get him going. Jonathan Agnew recalls an incident during the Fifth Test against Pakistan at The Oval in 1992 when Waqar Younis beat Mike Atherton outside the off stump.

'Fine delivery that,' commented Agnew.

'Yes,' replied Trevor Bailey, sitting alongside him. 'It's remarkable how he can whip it out just before tea.'

Total collapse of Johnners at the back of the box, making commentary on the next delivery, according to Agnew, 'a supreme effort'.

Brian Johnston:

If you're interviewing someone and they say something that isn't meant to be funny, at least on the radio you can hide your smile and – hopefully – suppress your giggles. But on television, if someone says something funny and it's not meant to be, you mustn't be seen to smile.

In 1952, when the Indians were here, I was down at Worcester. We always did the first match of the tour on television and inevitably it was raining, as it always did. About lunchtime my producer said, 'Right, go out under an umbrella and interview the Indian manager. We'll try and fill in some time.'

The Indian manager was a little man called Mr Gupte, a bit of a volatile chap. I don't know how much English he understood. Anyhow, I got him under the umbrella and said, 'Mr Gupte, have you got a good team?'

'Oh yes, we've got a very good team.'

'Really,' I said. 'Any good batsmen?'

'Seven very good batsmen.'

'What about the bowlers?'

'Six very good bowlers.'

I thought this was getting a bit boring and I'd better try another tack, so I said, 'What about yourself. Are you a selector?'

'No,' he replied, 'I'm a Christian!'

On the Mondays of a Test match at Lord's, the Queen always comes in the afternoon. It normally rains and there's hardly anybody there, but the teams are presented to her during the tea interval.

Robert Hudson was doing the commentary when the

New Zealanders were being presented to the Queen and he said, 'It's a great occasion for these Commonwealth teams. It's a moment they will always forget!'

Who am I to talk? At the royal wedding of the Prince of Wales and Lady Diana, I was on Queen Anne's statue just in front of St Paul's Cathedral. She was called Brandy Annie, I was told, because she was a bit keen on the grog.

So I had a marvellous view standing there, because all the coaches and carriages drew up about six feet below me. I could see the Queen, with a rug over her knees, being helped out and so on.

I looked over my shoulder and said, 'I can see Lady Diana coming up Ludgate Hill, in her coach with her two escorts. The coach will come below me here, a page will open the door and she will be greeted by her father, Earl Spencer. Then they will walk up the steps together, into the pavilion . . . I mean, cathedral!'

Henry Blofeld:

I'm often asked, what was your most embarrassing moment? I can answer that without any hesitation whatever. It was a long time ago now, I was working for the *Guardian,* and I was travelling around England at great speed. I went up to Old Trafford for a couple of days,

I went to Sheffield for another couple of days, then I went to Trent Bridge, and I stayed at one high-rise hotel after another. When I arrived in Nottingham I was booked into a new hotel that had just opened and I found myself on the ninth floor.

I was watching Nottinghamshire play Gloucestershire, and I'd had a little bit of a drink at Trent Bridge at the end of the day's cricket, so I caught a taxi back to the hotel. I had a bath, which is something I occasionally do, changed and put on a clean shirt and took a book down to dinner. I had an extremely good dinner with a very, very good bottle of wine. I remember it very well and I was rather surprised to find it there. So by the time I got to bed, I was 'very nicely thank-you', I suppose.

My trouble started because, ever since my keepers allowed me to, I have discarded pyjamas and I've always slept in the raw – I found it easier that way. So I got into bed and fell asleep, which was absolutely splendid, but I woke up soon afterwards at about a quarter to two to answer the call of nature.

Well, whereas most of us would flick on the switch at the side of the bed and negotiate our way into the bathroom that way, I thought all these high-rise buildings are exactly the same, the bathroom's in exactly the same place, look, no hands, I'll do it in the dark!

I got out of bed and I turned right and turned left and I found the handle of the door, turned it and went out. To my amazement the light was on, which rather surprised me. Then I looked and saw there was a wall about six feet in front of me. I thought, that's strange, there's no loo at all. Then I heard a great clunk behind me . . . you've guessed it, the door of my room had slammed shut and there I was, stark bollock naked on the ninth floor of this hotel in Nottingham.

It's quite a predicament. I really didn't know what to do. I was befuddled with sleep and my sense of judgement was gravely impaired. I wandered aimlessly up and down the corridor hoping for a staircase, but I couldn't find one. There was a lift, but I was rather apprehensive of the lift. Suddenly I saw, in a little nook outside a door, a tea tray; there was a pot on it and underneath the cup was a paper doily, folded into quarters.

I opened it out and held it in front of me and, without trying to show off in any way, it just about did duty. Really, in circumstances like that, there's not very much else one can do. I thought, it's nearly two o'clock in the morning; the night porter might get the thrill of a lifetime but he's a man, it should be all right. So I summoned the lift, which came up and I got into it. There were nine bedroom floors, I was on the top one, then it had buttons with the letters REST for the restaurant, BAR for the bar, and REC for reception.

With great care and precision, because my life depended upon it, I pressed the bottom button with REC on it. That was fine. The lift doors shut and we went down the first nine floors. Then quite suddenly the lift stopped. I thought this was rather strange. I looked up at the lights and it wasn't REC, it was REST.

I stood there shivering and the lift doors opened and to my horror, positively surging towards me, I saw eight ladies in long dresses and eight men in dinner jackets. And there I was! People thought it was terribly funny and came running to have a look – they were almost charging fifty pence a time – until eventually a funny little man came up and said, 'You look in a spot of bother!'

I said, 'How very swift of you to spot it.' Then I told him, 'The man I'm really after is the night porter,' and I realised as soon as I'd said it that I could have rephrased it to advantage.

He said, 'The night porter's over there. I'll go and get him. Keep the lift door open.' Well, that was a button at the top, so I had to do a very delicate operation, with one hand up pressing the button and the other one holding the doily, and to everyone's immense disappointment, I got it more or less right.

Then the night porter came and he thought I was a very suspicious character, but because I'd pressed the bottom button for reception, we went down together in the lift. People were running from floor to floor, so we had the whole thing again at the bar floor, and then at the bottom. Eventually, I got back to my room and the relief was tremendous.

The next morning I went to see the manager of the hotel to apologise, a chap called David Waite, I think his name was. I went into his office and said how sorry I was and he said he had heard what had happened. He said he wanted to ask me one particular question which rather puzzled him.

He said, 'I wondered why you held your doily where you did. You know, most people are recognisable by their faces!'

UMPIRES

Fred Trueman:

I have known a lot of good umpires and some who were *very* good. I have also encountered a few who don't come into either category. Rarely, though, have I encountered an umpire who wasn't, one way or another, a character.

Alec Skelding was a medium-fast bowler for Leicestershire from 1912 to 1929 and then an umpire for twenty-seven years. He did not retire until he was seventy-two and was still giving a smile to players in his last year.

His humour had a laconic, almost sly quality. I was talking to him once at Northampton just after I had made my first hundred, when he mentioned, 'I once got a hundred, you know.'

Surprised, because Alec's first-class average when he retired was 6.76, I replied, 'Did you really?'

'Aye,' said he. 'I started in April and I finished in September. But I did make a hundred runs!'

Brian Johnston:

I support umpires more than 100 per cent, if one can do such a thing. I think they have got a very difficult task and they do a marvellous job. But nowadays they are handicapped by the action replay, which makes their job absolutely impossible.

Umpires have to give a special hand signal if they want the third umpire to look at a replay on television. But soon after this was introduced, Dickie Bird gave the hand signal and the umpire in the pavilion called him up to say, 'Sorry, I was watching *Neighbours*!'

Talking of which, did you hear about the Irishman? Took a brilliant catch at third slip. Missed it on the action replay!

Dickie Bird:

One match at Chelmsford in 1996 will always stick in my mind. Essex were playing India, and during the match some building work was going on at the hospital just outside the ground. A massive mechanical hammer made a terrible noise throughout play. Boom, boom, boom, boom, it went. Non-stop. It was driving me crackers. You would think I could have coped, having umpired in India where the noise from the crowd is unbelievable, but this was something else. It went right through me, all day long.

Finally, I could stand it no longer, and I sent a message to the workmen asking if it would be possible for them not to make any noise during the hours of play. They could use the hammer from hell, I suggested, during our lunch and tea intervals, and in the evening after play had stopped for the day. Either that or put a muffler on the damn thing.

I hardly dare tell you the message I received back. But it began with an F and ended in off!

Brian Johnston:

Umpires are often treated very badly and I'll give you an example. It concerns Gilbert Harding. Many older people may remember Gilbert Harding on the television programme *What's My Line* – crusty, a brilliant brain, but very intolerant of other people's ignorance. He was a bit rude to them, but he used to send them flowers the next day!

When he was at Ampleforth School he was very short-sighted and very fat, so his headmaster said, 'All right, Harding, you can go for walks instead of playing cricket.'

Now this infuriated the young master, just down from Oxford, who took the cricket. He thought he would get his own back, which is always dangerous, and when he put the teams up on the board for the Masters against the Boys, underneath he put: Umpire – Gilbert Harding.

So Gilbert had to go and umpire and he was not too pleased about it at all. The master went in and hit the boys all around the field. He was 98 not out when a boy, bowling from Gilbert's end, hit him high in the chest and stifled an appeal for leg before wicket. But not before Gilbert had said, 'Out!'

This infuriated the young master who, as he went past Gilbert, said, 'Harding! I wasn't out! You weren't paying attention.'

Gilbert thought for a moment and said, 'On the contrary, sir. I *was* paying attention, and you weren't out!'

Fred Trueman:

We claim in England that our umpires are the best in the world, because the majority are former players – and I think that's right. They know the game from the inside and they can be relied upon to understand the problems.

It is a different matter in overseas countries, particularly in the West Indies and (usually for quite different reasons) Australia. There was an umpire called Kippins officiating on the 1959/60 tour of the West Indies who wouldn't give us a thing, and I remember asking him if one decision hadn't been very close. He replied, 'I couldn't give it because I couldn't see any stumps. He was covering the lot!'

In Trinidad every lbw appeal got the same answer: 'Too high.' Then Brian Statham hit a batsman very low on the pad and straight in front, but the umpire said, 'Not out.'

At the end of the over, Geoff Pullar, keeping his face straight, asked him, 'I suppose that was going *under* the stumps?'

He was told, 'Yes.'

Brian Johnston:

The famous umpire Bill Reeves was seldom at a loss for a reply. But even he was struck dumb when Surrey were playing Gloucestershire at Cheltenham and Alf Gover, Surrey's traditional number eleven, strode to the crease. Gover took up his stance ready to withstand the onslaught, scorning to take guard. Noting this somewhat irregular behaviour, Reeves said, 'Hey, Alf, don't you want your guard?'

'No, thanks,' said Alf, 'I've played here before!'

Henry Blofeld:

One of the great characters in my years in cricket was Bernard, the late Duke of Norfolk. His family have that wonderful cricket ground at Arundel, in West Sussex, where touring sides often play their first match. It is an absolutely glorious ground and he was a splendid man. He managed the 1962/63 England side in Australia when Ted Dexter was captain.

I was lucky enough to play at Arundel for the Eton Ramblers on a number of occasions and play usually began shortly after twelve o'clock, because the ducal family always went to the Roman Catholic cathedral in Arundel and did a bit of business on their knees before they came along. So it was about ten past twelve before the serious business was likely to be conducted.

Well, on this day, suddenly, up the hill in his Land Rover with the dogs barking in the back, came His Grace the Duke of Norfolk. But when the Duke arrived, there was only one umpire – the other umpire was late.

The Duke said, 'Don't worry, I'll go and get Meadows.'

Now Meadows was his butler, who did duty as umpire occasionally. So the Duke got into his Land Rover with the dogs in the back, drove back down the hill to the castle and went into the butler's pantry, where Meadows was pensively polishing the silver and probably having a second glass of port of the morning. He said, 'Meadows, you must come and umpire.'

So Meadows said, 'Very good, Your Grace,' and got his white coat. He got into the back of the Land Rover with the dogs, because he knew his place, and they went tootling back up the hill.

Well, His Grace the Duke of Norfolk got there in time. Meadows went out to umpire and the Duke rushed out to toss the coin, except he never rushed anywhere. It was always said by P.G. Wodehouse that Beech, who was the butler at Blandings, when he brought the tea out on the lawns in the afternoon, moved 'like a procession of one'. His Grace the Duke of Norfolk moved like a procession of one, I can assure you.

Anyway, his side won the toss and they batted and everything went perfectly swimmingly until quite late in the afternoon when they were about 240 for 7 and the eighth wicket fell. Now His Grace liked to bat. He didn't like the indignity of going in at number eleven, so he put himself in at number ten, where he was grossly overplaced.

The eighth wicket went down and there was a tremendous pause and then this very portly figure with an I Zingari waistcoat – not a jersey but a waistcoat – came out, his tummy leading the procession, and he found himself at the non-striker's end. Now His Grace loved not only to bat but to get off the mark and it was very important, if you wanted to be asked back as the visiting side the following year, that you allowed him to get off the mark. Sometimes it was not at all easy. I remember once, when I was keeping wicket, letting some byes through down the leg side. They went through for a very stately single and the umpire didn't signal the bye and

His Grace ruined it all by saying, 'I didn't hit it umpire, it was a bye.' So we had to start all over again.

Well, this time His Grace found himself at the non-striker's end and the chap at the striker's end was quite a decent cricketer, a young subaltern in some regiment. He was playing with His Grace for the first time and he didn't quite know what the form was. He was very, very keen and he played forward to the next ball. He hit it quite firmly to cover point's right hand and said, 'Yes! One!' and set off like a bat out of hell to the other end.

His Grace hadn't got the benefit of synchromesh and getting from a standing start into first gear meant an awful lot of crunching going on. Eventually, he got into first gear and he was just about going at the double, frantically trying to get into second, when the ball came thudding back into the wicket-keeper's gloves from cover point and the bails were taken off with a tremendous appeal.

Meadows was at square-leg and the Duke was nowhere to be seen. Meadows had a desperate moment. He thought, my goodness, my job, my pension, the family holiday . . . he saw the whole thing going up in smoke. He didn't know what to do and there was the Duke, puffing like a grampus in the other half of the pitch.

Eventually, Meadows drew himself up to his full height and, to no one in particular at square-leg, he said, 'His Grace is not in!'

Michael Atherton:

Dickie Bird was a popular but notoriously nervous umpire. Rain and bad weather seemed to follow him as inevitably as night follows day. During a Test match at Old Trafford in 1995, he astonished the natives by bringing off the players because the light was too bright! (It was reflecting off a greenhouse on the practice ground.)

Earlier in that match he interrupted play when he dropped the marbles that he used to count the number of deliveries that had been bowled. Play was halted momentarily while Dickie scrambled around on his hands and knees looking for his counters. 'I've lost me marbles! I've lost me marbles!' he cried. Most of us thought he had lost his marbles a long time ago.

Brian Johnston:

When I was in Australia in 1958/59 with Peter May's team, there was an umpire who wasn't very good. His name was McInnes and on the previous tour with Len Hutton he'd been very good indeed, but somehow he had failed. He made one or two bad mistakes.

Tom Crawford, who used to captain Kent second XI and was a great friend of mine, was talking to Don Bradman about this.

'The trouble with your umpires, Don,' he said, 'is that

they've never actually played Test cricket or even Shield cricket. They're not first-class cricketers. They've learnt all the laws and passed exams, but they don't know what goes on in the middle. At home, all our umpires are either Test players or county players.' (That was true then, but I think we've got some now who aren't.)

Don got very indignant about this. 'No, no,' he said. 'What about McInnes? He played for South Australia until his eyesight went.'

Then he realised what he'd said!

Dickie Bird:

They always blame me for bad light, don't they? It's always, 'That Dickie Bird!' They don't realise there's another umpire with me. I remember in a Test match at Old Trafford, Australia were batting and England were fielding. We all came off the field, all the players and the two umpires and we were walking up the members' enclosure to the dressing rooms.

There was a Lancashire member at the top of the members' enclosure, and he'd had so much to drink, he couldn't stand. He said, 'You're 'ere again, Bird, you're 'ere again. Every time you come to Old Trafford you're always bringing 'em off. Surely it's not bad light? The sun's shining.'

I said, 'No, sir, it's lunchtime!'

Brian Johnston:

There's a dreadful story that dear old Jim Laker used to tell about the Commonwealth tour in India in the 1950s, under Richie Benaud. There was himself, Bruce Dooland and George Tribe of Northants, an Australian, who bowled the chinaman – the left arm off-break.

George was getting the batsmen, time and time again, right up against the stumps, palpably out.

'Howzat!'

'Very close, Mr Tribe.'

'Howzat!!'

'Another inch and I'd have had to raise the finger, Mr Tribe.'

'Howzat!!!'

'Nearly, I had to give him the benefit of the doubt, Mr Tribe. Very difficult.'

George was getting fed up with this and off the sixth ball he more or less yorked the chap, who was right in front of his stumps. It *must* have hit the stumps and he turned round and said, 'What about that?'

The man began, 'Mr . . . ' and he got no further than that. George turned round, took him by the throat and said, 'Have another look!'

He said, 'You're right, Mr Tribe. He's out!'

David Lloyd:

The first game I stood in as a first-class umpire was at Fenners in April 1985 and the visitors were Essex. This was the Essex side of the early 1980s who carried all before them and existed on an exhausting diet of pranks and parties. It included characters such as Ray East, Keith Pont and John 'JK' Lever, a superb left-arm bowler who just enjoyed life to the full.

JK opened the bowling from my end when Essex took the field against Cambridge University and his first ball was a slow half-volley. Something not quite right, I thought, but exactly what did not register until the 'ball' struck the bat and disintegrated! Lever had bowled an orange.

Different players needed treating in different ways. With Ian Botham, the sensible umpire would cajole and indulge, without quite letting him run the game. I was standing in a Sunday League match at Taunton when Ian was batting against Wayne Daniel, Middlesex's West Indian fast bowler. It was a televised game and Both was milking the drama of a good finish.

We were midway through the last over and Somerset still required 12 to win. It seemed a long shot but Botham relished those and, as Daniel turned at the end of his run-up, he stood up from his stance and strolled halfway down the pitch, giving it a prod and calling out to me, 'Who are you backing?'

Only Botham could do this but I needed to keep the game moving. 'Three to go and twelve to win is a good contest,' I replied. 'Now, is there any chance of getting on with it, because *Songs of Praise* is next on and we're running late!'

Botham hit two sixes and Somerset won the game!

Brian Johnston:

Charlie Knott of Hampshire was bowling to Dusty Rhodes of Derbyshire and roared out a terrific appeal for a catch at the wicket: 'Howizee?'

To which Alec Skelding replied, 'Oh, he's not at all well and he was even worse last night!'

After another appeal for a run-out, which was a very close thing, Skelding declared, 'Gentlemen, it's a photo finish – and I haven't got time to develop the photo. Not out!'

During another match Johnny Wardle, the Yorkshire and England left-arm spin bowler, inquired of an umpire,

'You know, I think that ball would have hit the wicket. Where do you think it would have hit?'

'How should I know?' retorted the umpire. 'The gentleman's leg was in the way!'

Michael Atherton:

The Second Test against India at Lord's in 1996 was Dickie Bird's farewell match. On the first morning, I organised both teams to line up and applaud him on to the playing surface, and afterwards Alec Stewart and I followed the Indian team out. Bird was in tears. He hugged Mohammad Azharuddin, waved his hankie to all four corners of the ground and thanked me profusely. 'Eh lad, what an honour. I'm so grateful, Mike.'

Srinath bowled the first over of the match to me from Bird's end. He jagged the fifth ball down the Lord's slope and I shuffled across my crease and was trapped in front. Dickie's eyes were still red and he had scarcely wiped the tears from his cheeks, but he rightly waved his forefinger high above his head and shouted, practically bellowed, 'That's aht!'

Brian Johnston:

Surrey were playing Middlesex at The Oval and Bill Reeves was one of the umpires. Nigel Haig opened the bowling and Andrew Sandham went in first for Surrey. Sandham was not very tall and a ball from Haig hit him in the navel. There was a loud appeal.

'Not out,' said Reeves.

'Why not?' asked Haig.

'Too high,' said Reeves.

Haig went back to his mark muttering, possibly thinking that even if a ball hit a little chap like Sandham on the head, it couldn't be too high. A few deliveries later, a beautiful ball beat the batsman all ends up and hit Sandham on the pads.

'What about that one then?' yelled Haig.

'Not out,' said Reeves.

'Why not?' said Haig.

'Too low!' said Reeves . . . and that ended all arguments for that day!

Fred Trueman:

One of the great umpiring remarks of all time must be that of Arthur Jepson, formerly of Notts, who was standing at Old Trafford during that celebrated limited-overs match against Gloucestershire, which went on until a few seconds before 9 p.m.

It was late in the day when Jackie Bond, the Lancashire captain, came in to bat. The lights were on in the pavilion and in Warwick Road station; the moon and stars were clearly visible in the night sky. Bond looked at Jepson and asked, 'What are we doing, playing in this light?'

Jepson replied, tartly, 'What about the light?'

'Well, it's pretty dark, isn't it?' retorted Jackie, staunchly.

'What's that up there?' questioned Jepson, gazing up at the sky.

Bond responded, 'Well, that's what I mean – it's the moon, isn't it?'

Jepson returned, 'And how far away is *that*?'

Bond thought for a minute, and replied, 'It's about two hundred and sixty thousand miles, isn't it?'

Jepson ended the conversation with, 'Then how bloody far do you want to see?'

Brian Johnston:

When Harold Larwood played against Wilfred Rhodes for the first time, he noticed that the Yorkshire batsman, when he was taking his stance, had the front of his left foot cocked off the ground. 'What's he doing that for?' said Lol to umpire Bill Reeves.

'Oh, he always stands like that,' said the umpire.

'He won't to me,' said Larwood, and rushing up to the wicket bowled a full toss, which landed with a mighty crack on Rhodes' toes. 'How's that?' yelled Larwood.

'Bloody painful, I should think!' said Reeves.

Dickie Bird:

I was umpiring at square-leg in a county game at Derbyshire and Devon Malcolm, who normally wears glasses but opts for contact lenses when playing, was fielding on the fine-leg boundary. The ball was played down towards him and he raced round – well, ambled is probably a better description, because Devon was no Linford Christie – in order to field it. He threw it in and it hit me smack between the shoulder blades.

I wondered what the hell had happened. I went down like a pricked balloon. Devon ran up to me, concern written all over his face. He picked me up, dusted me down, and muttered, 'Sorry, Dickie, I thought you were the stumps.'

'Dev,' I said, 'I know your eyesight isn't brilliant, mate, but I can't believe that. Whenever did you come across stumps wearing a white cap?'

SLEDGING

Barry Johnston:

During the 2001 Ashes series, the young Leicestershire bowler James Ormond came out to bat in the Fifth Test at The Oval. Australia had declared their first innings on 641 for 4 and Ormond, making his Test debut at the age of twenty-four, had taken just one wicket for 115 runs. He was greeted by Mark Waugh, younger twin brother of the Australian captain Steve Waugh, with the remark, 'Mate, what are you doing out here? There's no way you're good enough to play for England.'

Ormond retorted, 'Maybe not, but at least I'm the best player in my family!'

Richie Benaud:

The closest I reckon I got to experiencing sledging was during the Fourth Ashes Test at Old Trafford in 1956. This will always be remembered as 'Laker's Match' after the England off-spinner finished with the amazing figures of 19 for 90. There were some very unhappy Australians in that match, in the main because we had the feeling we were playing on a rather unusual pitch, and we were looking at defeat, which never actually makes one happy.

Well, you would be unhappy too if you were thrashed, one of the opposition bowlers took 19 wickets in the match and the ball turned square for much of the game. Additionally, the rain fell on either side of the ground on the last day, but none fell on it. You would also be unhappy if you were the bowler who took only one wicket of the twenty little Australians to fall. Jim Burke was the generous batsman who was the victim of Tony Lock.

On the final afternoon I was engaged in some prudent 'gardening' against 'Lockie', patting down the pitch, sometimes not quite ready to face up, so much so that one prominent English administrator, sitting alongside a very prominent Australian administrator, said grimly that, because of the gardening, I should never at any time in the future hold a position of responsibility in an Australian team.

Out in the centre at Old Trafford, Colin McDonald and I were battling our way through to the tea interval and, in the last over, Tony bowled from what was then the Warwick Road End. I played forward firmly to a half-volley and it went to the bowler's left hand.

Great fielder, Lockie, and a very good and accurate throwing arm in either the infield or farther out. He gathered this ball and it rocketed into Godfrey Evans's left glove, alongside my left ear, and floating down the pitch came, 'Tap that one down, you little bastard!'

Barry Johnston:

Ian Botham was the target of a classic sledge by the Australian wicket-keeper Rodney Marsh during the thrilling 1981 Ashes series. As the England all-rounder took guard in one of the Test matches, Marsh tried to put him off by saying, 'So, how's your wife, and my kids?'

Botham silenced him with the brilliant reply, 'The wife's fine . . . but the kids are retarded!'

Michael Atherton:

During my second Test match, at The Oval in 1989, I had my first taste of Australian sledging. They tended to pick on the youngest, or those they considered the weakest. Merv Hughes probably thought I was both young and weak and he snarled at me constantly through his ludicrous moustache. He was all bristle and bullshit and I couldn't make out what he was saying, except that every sledge ended with 'arsewipe'. I smiled and shrugged and saved my energy.

Four years later, in the First Test against Australia at Old Trafford, I made 19 and 25 and I was once again a verbal target for Merv Hughes. I had not played against him since the 1990/91 Ashes series in Australia and had missed his kind and gentle countenance. As I nicked the first ball for four through third man the moustache hissed at me, 'Jesus Christ, you've not got any better in two f***ing years!' And then as I ran past him, just in case I had forgotten his calling card, he added, '. . . arsewipe!'

Barry Johnston:

During a county championship match between Glamorgan and Somerset, Greg Thomas was bowling to Viv Richards. The Glamorgan paceman had managed to beat the bat a couple of times and was feeling rather pleased with himself. He taunted Richards, 'It's red, round and weighs about five ounces, in case you were wondering.'

The next delivery, Viv Richards took an almighty heave at the ball and smashed it straight out of the ground and into a river – after which he turned to Thomas and said, 'Greg, you know what it looks like. Now go and find it!'

Shane Warne:

England have generally begun each Ashes series against us with plenty to say for themselves. The problem is that if you start sledging without being able to back up your words with performances, then it soon loses its effect. There is no point threatening this and that if you're going to be rissoled inside three days. Merv Hughes in particular used to relish the Ashes contests, and usually reserved a special word for Graeme Hick. England used to say the odd word here and there, but nothing that badly affected any of us.

On the other hand, they could be susceptible themselves. My dismissal of Nasser Hussain, in the first Carlton & United final match at Sydney in 1999, springs to mind. England needed less than 50 to win, with six wickets and 10 overs remaining, and Hussain was going pretty well. He had the reputation of being a little on the fiery side and I decided the only way we could win from that position was to tempt him into doing something silly.

At that stage he was not a regular feature of their one-day side, so I tried to goad him by talking him through the game. I would say things like, 'This is where it's crucial not to get out, Nass,' or, 'Don't let your team-mates down now, mate.'

This went on for a couple of overs and he said a bit back, so it was game on. When he ran down the pitch and hit me over the top I clapped him and said, 'Great stuff, Nass, that's the way to do it.' At the end of the over his face was red and you could almost see the steam coming out of his ears. I knew then that the ploy might work.

Lo and behold, in my next over he ran down the track, and was stumped by Adam Gilchrist about three yards out of his ground. With new batsmen in, we had a chance. Adam Hollioake followed next ball, and we ended up winning the game. It was one of the few occasions sledging worked – remember, pick your moment!

Barry Johnston:

In 1989 Merv Hughes was bowling to England batsman Robin Smith during the Second Ashes Test at Lord's. After Smith had played and missed several times, Hughes snarled, 'You can't f***ing bat!'

A few balls later, Smith smacked Hughes to the boundary and called out to the fiery Australian, 'Hey, Merv, we make a fine pair. I can't f***ing bat and you can't f***ing bowl!'

The Second Ashes Test in 2005 has been described as the most exciting Test match of all time. Having been soundly beaten by the Australians at Lord's, England fought back at Edgbaston to win by just two runs in a thrilling, nail-biting finish. The abiding image of the game was the picture of Andrew Flintoff crouching with his arm around a despondent Brett Lee, congratulating the Aussie tailender on his valiant effort. It was hailed by the media and the general public as the epitome of chivalry and sportsmanship – but all was not quite as it seemed. A few months later Flintoff admitted, 'When I put my arm around him, the exact words I used were, "It's one–one, you Aussie bastard!"'

Michael Vaughan:

Shane Warne's record speaks for itself. He comes at you even when he is not bowling, standing at first slip chirping away. He is a very psychological player and tries to get into a batsman's head, forever trying to talk players out. Not only that, but he tells you how he is going to get you out. Rather than speaking to the captain in a discreet manner, he will make sure you can hear him. He is one of their best chirpers. He will say things like, 'Don't worry, he's going to hit one straight to gully in a minute.' Comments like that I can just laugh off, but with an inexperienced player it might work, because Warne is quite clever at it.

Not all his plans follow the script. I remember once in Adelaide, he was bowling at Nasser Hussain and said, 'I'm going to throw one up, and you'll drive and edge it.' Two overs later he lobbed one up and, sure enough, Nasser edged it, but just as Warne was about to celebrate and say told you so, Damien Martyn dropped the catch!

Barry Johnston:

Glenn McGrath was bowling to the Zimbabwe number eleven, Eddo Brandes, a heavily built chicken farmer who became famous in 1997 when he took a hat-trick in a one-day international against England. Brandes, nick-named 'Chicken George', was flailing away with his bat, hardly making any contact with the ball, but the Australians could not prise him from the crease. After a few overs, McGrath got so frustrated that he walked up to the Zimbabwean batsman and inquired, 'Why are you so fat?'

Quick as a flash, Brandes replied, 'Because every time I make love to your wife, she gives me a biscuit!'

Andrew Flintoff:

During the First Test against the West Indies at Lord's in 2004, there was a comical moment with my old friend Tino Best. We had got off to a bad start earlier that year in the Caribbean when he played a trick on me in the Second Test at Trinidad, which I didn't find very funny. I had just walked out to bat and took guard ready for him to run in. He came charging in, like he does, and bowled and at first I thought it must have been a beamer because I didn't see it come out of his hand. I was expecting to get hit on the head at any moment because I just hadn't picked it up. But he thought it was a huge joke because he had run in without a ball in his hand. I'm the first one to enjoy a laugh and a joke on the field and there are some things you can do, but that was just not one of them. I didn't find it funny at all.

Four months later it was payback time at Lord's. I was standing at slip and Tino was trying to hit Ashley Giles out of the ground and swiping and missing. I couldn't help myself saying, 'Mind the windows, Tino!' And he just couldn't resist. He had to try to smash Giles again and of course missed altogether. The ball went straight through to wicket-keeper Geraint Jones and Tino was stumped by a mile. Now that *was* a good laugh!

Barry Johnston:

A few weeks before the start of the 2005 Ashes series Australian all-rounder Shane Watson learned that his fiancée, professional dancer Kym Johnson, had left him for the hunky TV presenter Tom Williams, her partner on the Australian television show *Dancing with the Stars*.

In June, England were playing Australia in their first NatWest Series one-day match at Bristol when Kevin Pietersen smashed Watson over the boundary for an almighty six, depositing the ball ten rows back, on his way to an unbeaten 91 and an England victory. At the end of the over the blond, spiky-haired Watson started to give Pietersen a dose of the verbals, until KP shut him up by saying, 'You're just upset because no one loves you any more!'

Even Aussie captain Ricky Ponting chuckled at that one as Watson stomped off to square-leg.

Kevin Pietersen:

Sledging, or mental disintegration as the Australians like to call it, is a feature of cricket that fascinates people. What some people don't realise is that sledging can be very humorous too. It's not all swearing and unpleasantness, believe me. What I always try to remember is that it's just play-acting.

Before the 2005 Ashes series there was a triangular one-day series between England, Australia and Bangladesh. We won our first two matches but Australia started to find their feet in the day/night game that we played at Durham when they beat us by 57 runs after we had made a very poor start with the bat. Even in defeat, though, we managed to score a few psychological points and have a good laugh in the process, when Darren Gough decided to have a bit of fun at the expense of Aussie all-rounder Shane Watson. The papers had been full of stories of the Aussies being haunted by ghosts at their Lumley Castle hotel, which overlooked the ground, and Goughy found the opportunity too hard to resist. When Watson, who apparently had not been too keen to be alone in his 'haunted' room, came in to bat, Darren

crept up behind him and, in true Scooby-Doo style, went 'Whooooh!'

Barry Johnston:

Shane Watson was so spooked by tales of seven-hundred-year-old ghosts at the Lumley Castle hotel that he had to sleep on the floor in Brett Lee's room. England spinner Ashley Giles chortled, 'The thought of big, strapping Shane Watson asking Brett Lee if he could kip on his floor because he was scared of a ghost shows the Aussies are not as tough as some people make out.' When Watson came in to bat at the Riverside Ground next day, Darren Gough welcomed him with the words, 'Don't worry, you can sleep in *my* bed tonight!'

By the end of the 1990/91 Ashes series in Australia, Phil Tufnell had become a cult figure among the Australian supporters – but for all the wrong reasons. The Middlesex spinner made his Test debut in the Second Ashes Test at Melbourne on Boxing Day but it was an inauspicious start to his Test career. England lost by eight wickets and Tufnell failed to take a wicket or score a run in either innings.

Things got even worse a few days later in a World Series day/night match at the Sydney Cricket Ground. The Australian Waugh brothers, Steve and Mark, were batting when they mixed up the call for a run and both ended up at the striker's end. Eddie Hemmings lobbed the ball gently to Phil Tufnell standing at the bowler's end, for what looked like an easy run-out, and Steve Waugh started to walk off. But not only did a nervous Tufnell fumble and drop the ball, he then picked it up and hurled it so wildly that it missed the stumps by a mile. Unable to believe his luck, Steve Waugh jogged safely back to his crease while the whole Sydney Cricket Ground erupted with laughter, especially when Tufnell's ineptitude was replayed over and again, in slow motion, on the giant screen.

As the series progressed, so Tufnell's fielding went from bad to worse, and he admits that he spent most of his time in the field praying that the ball would not come anywhere near him. But the Australian crowds loved him for it and a group of supporters even founded the Phil Tufnell Fielding Academy. Phil was on the receiving end of a torrent of friendly abuse, but his favourite was when someone in the crowd called out, 'Hey Tufnell, lend me your brain, I'm building an idiot!'

Dickie Bird:

Merv Hughes was never short of a word or three. On one occasion Javed Miandad, of Pakistan, found himself out-manoeuvred by Merv during a Test match in which there was considerable needling. Merv had a go at Miandad, who jabbered back nineteen to the dozen, eventually snarling, 'Oh, get back to your mark, you bus conductor.'

Merv bridled. The old moustache started quivering, his nostrils flared and he stomped back muttering dark curses under his breath. He tore in like a man possessed for the next delivery and clean bowled Miandad. As the Pakistani tucked his bat under his arm and took off his helmet to make his way back to the pavilion, Merv called out, 'Tickets please!'

Barry Johnston:

In the Centenary Test at Melbourne in 1977 David Hookes was making his Test debut for Australia. As he made his way out to the crease, the twenty-one year old was met by the England captain, South-African-born Tony Greig, who asked the fair-haired young batsman, 'When are your balls going to drop, sonny?'

Hookes replied, 'I don't know, but at least I'm playing cricket for my own country!'

During a Test match, Fred Trueman forced an edge from the batsman and it flew straight towards Raman Subba Row standing at first slip. Not only did Subba Row fail to catch it, but the ball went right through his legs and carried on down to the third-man boundary. Trueman was silently fuming as he trudged back to his mark. At the end of the over, Subba Row, looking suitably embarrassed, went up to the bowler and said apologetically, 'Sorry, Fred. I should've kept my legs together.'

Trueman snorted, 'Not you, son. Your mother should've!'

Michael Atherton:

In Melbourne on the 1998/99 Ashes tour, Mark Butcher had moved down to number three from his usual opening berth, but each innings he was in by the second over. Ian Healy, the Australian wicket-keeper, gleefully piped up, 'Not much different at number three, is it, Butch!'

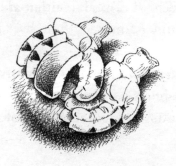

Barry Johnston:

During a tour match in South Africa in early 1994, Merv Hughes was bowling to Hansie Cronje, the South African captain, who was hitting him all over the ground. After the ball had crossed the boundary rope for the umpteenth time, Merv finally lost his cool. He strode down the pitch, stood in front of Cronje and let out the most enormous fart. Glaring at the South African captain, Merv snarled, 'Try hitting that for six!'

It was about five minutes before the players had stopped laughing and the game could continue.

After making his Test debut in 2006, Monty Panesar quickly became a cult hero among England cricket fans. The left-arm spinner was the first Sikh to play cricket for England and his exuberant celebrations every time he took a wicket, coupled with his often inept fielding and batting performances, endeared him to spectators and to the public at large. He soon acquired the nickname 'The Sikh of Tweak', although Henry Blofeld once called him Monty Python by mistake on *Test Match Special*.

Before the 2006/07 Ashes series in Australia, Monty went to see a sports psychologist to prepare himself for the tour. He was worried about the sledging he might receive from the Australian players, and also the crowds, because of his poor batting and fielding. His session with the mind doctor seems to have worked. When he was asked what he thought about the Aussie sledging, Monty replied cheerfully, 'Sledging? I'm just glad they've heard of me!'

Richie Benaud:

For straightforward repartee I've always liked David Steele, who was brought into the England team in 1975 by Tony Greig after he took over the captaincy from Mike Denness. When, in the first innings, Barry Wood was lbw to Dennis Lillee with the score at 10 and the very grey-haired right-hander from Northamptonshire arrived in the centre, it was to hear someone chiding Dennis for not having mentioned his father was playing in the match.

It is said Steele looked straight past the Australian wicket-keeper Rodney Marsh and muttered, 'Take a good look at this arse of mine; you'll see plenty of it this summer.' Test innings of 50, 45, 73, 92, 39 and 66, and then a century for Northants against Australia later in the summer, made it a nice little story, some say apocryphal – except that, for whatever extraordinary selection quirk, he never played against Australia again!

Barry Johnston:

The South African batsman Daryll Cullinan developed a phobia about playing against the leg-spin bowling of Shane Warne, who always seemed to get him out cheaply. In fact, before the South Africans toured Australia in 1997, there was an article in an Australian newspaper in which Cullinan revealed that he had seen a psychiatrist to help him overcome his fear of Shane Warne and the Aussies. Warne couldn't believe it.

The day of the First Test at Melbourne finally dawned. Adam Bacher fell to a fine slip catch by Mark Taylor and Cullinan walked out gingerly to the crease. Warne let him take guard before saying, 'Daryll, I've waited so long for this moment and I'm going to send you straight back to that leather couch.' A couple of balls later Warne bowled him for a duck. Cullinan was more embarrassed than anything else, but those words had clearly unsettled him, and he took no further part in the Test series.

However Cullinan got his revenge eighteen months later. During their 1999 World Cup encounter at Headingley, Warne again welcomed the unfortunate Cullinan to the crease by saying that he had been waiting months for the joy of renewing their acquaintance. This time Cullinan replied quickly, 'Yeah, and it looks like you've spent most of that time eating!'

Even when he was not playing against Australia, Daryll Cullinan could not escape from Warne's shadow because he was well known for being Warne's bunny. The New Zealand wicket-keeper Adam Parore once greeted the South African, carefully playing the first ball from Chris Harris, with a loud cry of, 'Bowled, Warnie!'

Andrew Strauss:

Steve Kirby, the nutty Gloucester opening bowler, once famously sledged Mike Atherton by saying he had seen better players in his fridge!

Barry Johnston:

England were playing Australia and Nasser Hussain was at the crease. Steve Waugh, the Aussie captain, walked over to Ricky Ponting and told him, 'Field at silly point. I want you right under his nose.'

On hearing this, the wicket-keeper Ian Healy blurted out, 'That would be anywhere inside a three-mile radius!'

Nasser couldn't stop himself laughing. He didn't find it quite so funny when he was out three balls later!

Sometimes sledging has the opposite effect to the one intended. After their Ashes triumph in 2005 the members of the England team were each awarded the MBE, including Paul Collingwood, although he played in only one Test and made just 7 runs.

A year later it was a different story as England were whitewashed 5–0 in Australia. In the Fifth Test at the Sydney Cricket Ground in January 2007, Shane Warne was making his final Test appearance. Early in his innings he gloved a ball off Monty Panesar and was caught behind, but umpire Aleem Dar turned down the appeal. After that, Warne started to receive some heavy sledging from the England fielders, led by Paul Collingwood, who was heard to say, 'Did you get stuck into all the pies and soft drinks over Christmas, Shane?'

Warne responded, 'You aren't putting me off, you know. You're making me concentrate even more.'

At one point the constant chirping from the England fielders became so animated that umpire Billy Bowden had to intervene, but it backfired on England. Warne, now fired-up by all the banter, smashed 71 off just 65 balls to put Australia firmly in command of the match.

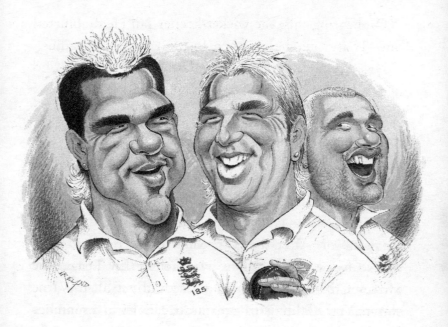

As he sent another six sailing into the stands, Warne turned to Collingwood and said, 'You got an MBE right? For scoring seven at The Oval. How embarrassing is that?'

The undisputed winner on points – Mr Shane Warne.

CLUB CRICKET

Brian Johnston:

I wasn't a bad wicket-keeper and I wasn't a good one. I was just so-so in club cricket, but I loved it and I played an awful lot. After the war, when I joined the BBC, I was so lucky because there was no Sunday League or whatever it's called now. So you could get all the Test players, and all the visiting teams, to play charity matches on a Sunday.

I kept wicket for fifteen years after the war to all the great bowlers – Lindwall, Laker, Lock, Trueman, Miller, Bedser – you think of anyone, I kept wicket to them. Great fun for me, not much fun for them!

They were very kind to me, but I came down to earth with a bump. I began to think I was getting rather good, playing in these matches, and we went to the Dragon School at Oxford where Richie Benaud, the Australian captain, was playing and I was keeping wicket. He was bowling his flipper and his googly and his top spinner and his leg-break. I was reading them all well . . . they all went for four byes, but I read them well!

Then the last chap came in and Richie bowled him a tremendous leg-break. This chap went right down the pitch, missed the ball, and it came into my gloves. With all my old speed, so I thought, I flicked off the bails, just like that, and the umpire said, 'Out!'

It was a great moment for me, a club cricketer, stumping someone off the Australian captain. So I was looking a bit pleased with myself when I walked off the field and the bursar of the school came up and said, 'Jolly well stumped.'

'Thanks very much,' I said.

'Yes,' he went on, 'I'd also like to congratulate you on the sporting way you tried to give him time to get back!'

Michael Parkinson:

I used to play cricket with a man called Billy Hopkinson who made John McEnroe look like the best-behaved athlete in the world. Whenever he was given out lbw his team-mates would evacuate the dressing room, taking all their gear with them, before Billy returned to vent his rage on whatever he could lay his hands on. The main sufferers were the unfortunate batsmen who were at the crease immediately after Billy was given out.

All they could do was stand and watch as their gear came through the dressing-room window to be followed by Billy's gear, the wooden benches, the matting carpet and, on very bad days, the large brown teapot that the tea ladies borrowed from the church hall, which was only used for funerals and cricket matches.

As befitted a world-class tantrum-thrower, in the field Billy Hopkinson could produce an outburst at the correct tactical time. He was the best 'ooher' and 'aaher' I ever played with and also the best running commentator.

On arriving at the wicket, the new batsman would find Billy staring thoughtfully at a spot just short of a length. 'Looks nasty to me that does,' he'd say, sometimes going down on his hands and knees to calculate the size of an imaginary ridge.

'I've never fancied this wicket since our Albert got his nose broke. Made a right mess it did. You could hear the crack a mile away. Off a slow bowler, too,' he would say, while the batsman tried to look cool.

From that point on, the batsman's survival depended on his ability to concentrate on his game while being subjected to a barrage of propaganda from Billy at first slip. Any ball that went past the bat would bring an anguished 'ooooh' or 'aaaah' from Billy. It didn't matter if it was a yard outside the off stump, Billy reacted as if it had passed through the wickets.

Not surprisingly, Billy wasn't the most popular cricketer in the district. There were many players who disliked being bowled out while in the middle of an argument with Billy about whether or not the previous ball had shaved the wickets.

One player dismissed in such a manner decided on swift justice. Instead of returning to the pavilion he set off after Billy waving his bat like a club. But Billy was soon three fields away and wisely he took no further part in the game, spending the afternoon at home and sending his missus down to the ground for his kit.

I only saw him beaten at his own game once and that was by a dark, squat little man who answered everything Billy said about him with a tiny smile, a neat bow of the head and a 'thank you very much'. Finally, Billy could endure it no longer. At the end of the over he confronted the batsman.

'Aye oop, mister. I've been talking to thee all afternoon and tha's said nowt. What's up?'

The batsman looked at him, smiled, bowed and said, 'Thank you very much.'

Billy turned in despair to the other batsman. 'What the bloody hell's up wi' thi' mate?' he demanded.

'Didn't tha' know, Billy? He doesn't speak English. He's Polish,' the batsman said.

'Polish!' said Billy. 'Polish! What's a bloody Polisher doing playing cricket?'

He was silent for the rest of the afternoon, only occasionally muttering the odd obscenity about foreigners. It never occurred to him that there was something very odd about a Pole who spoke no English and yet played cricket well. He was too busy fuming to consider that he might have been conned by a superior foe.

None of us dared put the point to him and indeed we were glad we hadn't for otherwise we would have missed those marvellous moments in subsequent matches when, giving a new batsman the ritual spiel, he would look at him and say, 'I suppose tha' speaks English, lad?'

Brian Johnston:

A man, whose wife was in hospital expecting a baby, telephoned one afternoon to see what the news was. By mistake he got the local cricket ground. When he asked what was the latest position the reply came back, 'There are seven out already – and the last two were ducks!'

Barry Johnston:

Johnners loved playing cricket but he could never take it seriously for too long. George Thorne probably bowled more balls to Brian than anyone else during their school-days at Eton. According to Thorne, Brian was usually worth two extra wickets to him because he would pretend to encourage the batsmen from behind the stumps. 'Don't worry,' Brian would reassure an incoming batsman, 'Thorne's no good. He'll never get you out!'

The batsman would relax, and a few balls later he would be clean bowled.

When batting, because of his speed as a runner, Brian would always go for a quick single and his fellow batsmen had to be on their toes. If a ball was going to the left hand of a right-handed fielder, Brian would often shout, 'Come five!' which so confused the fielder that he would return the ball wildly and Brian would get overthrows.

On one occasion, Brian was batting with the Earl of Hopetoun at the other end, a boy who was slightly overweight and not very fit. Brian hit a ball towards the boundary and yelled at his partner to run. By the time Hopetoun was turning to start his second run Brian had already completed two and they ran down the wicket together. Brian soon left him behind and by the time he had run four poor Hopetoun was still only halfway through his third. By now the whole field was helpless with laughter and when the ball was finally thrown in to the bowler's end no one could decide which batsman was out.

Thorne says there was never a dull moment when Brian was playing. In 1931 during their first year at Oxford, the two of them played together in an Eton Ramblers match against Windsor House Park, who were mainly cricket-playing Eton masters. Thorne took six wickets in quick succession, all of them clean bowled.

After the fourth wicket Brian called out, 'Can't you think of anything else to do? It's hard work picking up these stumps!'

Brian Johnston:

I always like the original umpire story of village cricket, where the home umpire, as they were always called, was umpiring against the visiting side. Their best batsman was hit somewhere high up on the chest, there was an appeal for lbw and the local umpire gave 'out' to the home side.

As he went past, this distinguished-looking batsman said, 'I wasn't out, umpire.'

The umpire gave the traditional reply, 'Well, you look in Wednesday's *Gazette* and see.'

This chap said, '*You* look. I'm the editor!'

Dickie Bird:

While speaking at a dinner in Surrey, I heard a lovely story that concerned Berkhamsted CC. One day they were playing Chesham, and the Berkhamsted captain, who had never scored a century in his life, was 98 not out. His team needed 18 to win and there were still a few wickets in hand, with plenty of time left. He found himself with a new partner, a young lad called Jamie

Brook, who was making his first appearance for the club. Brook promptly smashed three sixes to win the match, robbing his despairing captain of his long-awaited century. The youngster was dropped for the next match and never played for the team again!

Brian Johnston:

A batsman was playing in a very important match when he saw a funeral passing the cricket ground and he held up his hand to stop the bowler from bowling. Then he removed his cap and stood at the wicket with his head bowed in silence until the funeral had passed. Afterwards he replaced his cap and continued batting, hitting the next ball for six, clean out of the ground. At the end of the over the wicket-keeper said to him, 'That was a very nice gesture of yours, paying such respect to the funeral procession.'

'Well,' said the batsman, 'I've been married to her for thirty years . . . it was the least I could do!'

Barry Johnston:

The astronomer Sir Patrick Moore, presenter of *The Sky At Night* for more than fifty years, used to enjoy playing cricket for the Lord's Taverners charity teams and for his village team at Selsey in West Sussex. He was a moderately successful bowler, thanks to his 'medium-paced leg-breaks with a long, leaping, kangaroo-type action'. His batting, however, was another story. A firm number eleven bat, in a playing career that extended over half a century he achieved the superb batting average of 0.8 runs an innings. In his best season, in 1948, he scored only one run and that was from a dropped catch. That year he shattered the existing record for the most consecutive ducks when he ran up a magnificent eighteen on the trot.

Moore put this remarkable feat down to having only two strokes, 'a cow shot to leg' and 'a desperate forward swat', which he used in strict rotation. Perhaps more importantly, although the astronomer normally sported a monocle in his right eye, he did not wear spectacles when batting. Moore once observed, 'Someone said it wouldn't make any difference if I wore binoculars!'

Harry Thompson: Penguins Stopped Play

The whole Captain Scott obsession was down, in the first place, to Robert. Marcus, an old school friend whom I'd known since I was ten, had arrived at Oxford University at the same time as me, and had fetched up on a landing in Worcester College with two other first-years, Terence and Robert.

Marcus and I had not been allowed to play cricket by

our colleges. Robert was good enough for his college, but couldn't be arsed to get up early enough for the practice sessions. Terence – well, Terence couldn't play cricket either, but he'd happily tag along with the rest of us if we felt like doing something about it. There was only one option open to us. We would start our own cricket team.

We would play fantasy village-green cricket against horny-handed blacksmiths, not spotty, serious-minded student cricket. And we would name our team after Captain Scott, because he came second, and because he did so in the right spirit. We would call it the Captain Scott Invitational XI, because anybody – absolutely *anybody* – could invite themselves to play. It didn't matter if they'd never played before, or if they were complete rubbish – just as long as they did their best.

Our first task was to recruit some more players, which we did by means of a classified ad. None of the motley bunch that assembled in my college room that wintry night had ever played the game before, except Tom Cairns, a would-be actor in impossibly tight leather trousers, who assured us that he was a rather nifty bowler. Now, when somebody tells you that they're rather good at any sport, it means they're either (a) a five times Olympic gold medallist or (b) utterly useless. We took Cairns at face value – none of us had ever seen trousers that tight before – and it was only when his bowling average sailed past the 100 mark in mid-season that we realised he too was a member of the latter category.

Our first game, against the village of Bladon, north of Oxford, could not have conformed to the pictured idyll more closely: a blazing mid-May day of the kind that comes around once every hundred years or so, a gorgeous wooden-railed pitch at the bottom of a hill beneath the stately bulk of Blenheim Palace, sheep grazing along the boundary, a pond glittering between the trees, and an opposition comprised entirely of gnarled Mummerset yokels. One of our players asked for ice in the pub.

'Oice? For the Captain Scott XI? Har! Har! Har!' The entire pub rocked with laughter.

'No, I really would like some ice,' he explained, whereupon the pub fell about again, a procedure that was to be repeated several times before he retreated in disarray.

It was only when the game began that it finally dawned on us that we didn't have the slightest idea what we were doing. I made the deeply humiliating personal discovery that my own cricketing ability roughly approximated to that of Mother Teresa of Calcutta. I couldn't bat, bowl or field, let alone captain. Batting, for instance, bore no resemblance whatsoever to the childishly easy activity portrayed on television. If you've never tried it, imagine trying to hit a swerving cherry tomato travelling at 100 m.p.h, wielding a broom handle.

After Bladon had declared on a comfortable 250 for 4

(a huge score for a village match, had we but known it), we proceeded serenely enough to 58, courtesy of Robert and Tom Cairns, who could bat a bit even if he couldn't bowl. Thereafter Robert was given out lbw by Terence (incorrectly, as it turned out, for he hadn't read the rules) and the whole thing fell to pieces. Robert chased Terence into the trees with a cricket stump. The next eight men scored five runs between them. Five of us made 0. I did indeed manage to whack my first ball for miles and miles. Unfortunately, I did so vertically, and was caught when it finally returned earthward, having disturbed several Russian satellites. We were all out for 63, and lost by 187 runs.

And so the newborn Captain Scott XI went about its business. We quickly became known as the worst team in Oxfordshire, utterly inept in every department. In one match we were all out for 7, in another for 8. I hit every ball I received vertically upward, and by the end of the season had mustered the princely total of one run. My only consolation was that Marcus had accumulated 0. Even our wicket-keeping – this was Robert's job – was a hopeless mess, because Robert refused to collect any ball travelling down the leg side of the wicket, lest the need to scurry across compromised his dignity. Such leg byes frequently accounted for a quarter of the opposition total, usually more than our whole team had managed between them.

Robert was discreetly replaced behind the stumps by Terence, who was no better; indeed, Lot's wife would have been more agile. Terence did, however, afford us all some amusement when he took a particularly fast delivery in the testicles, after which it was discovered that he had not been wearing a box. Once he had finished writhing around in agony he was offered one, but declined, as there was only one ball left in the innings, and such a thing was hardly likely to happen twice in two balls. You've guessed it. That is, of course, precisely what happened next. The first time, he had received some rudimentary medical attention. The second time, he was left to roll around in agony by himself, as the rest of us were rolling around alongside him, helpless with laughter.

Brian Johnston:

When cricketers meet they inevitably swap cricket stories and I heard this favourite back in the 1960s. The Church of England received a challenge to a cricket match at Lord's from the Roman Catholics. The Archbishop of Canterbury was naturally keen to know what sort of chance his side would have before he took up the challenge, so he conferred with the Reverend David Sheppard, the former England captain, who recommended acceptance only if the Church of England could obtain the services of England batsman Ken Barrington. The Archbishop took his advice. He summoned Barrington, specially ordained him, and immediately accepted the challenge.

At half-past one on the day of the match he rang up Lord's to ask David Sheppard the score.

'What's our score?'

'I'm sorry, Your Grace, but we are forty-four for nine.'

'How dreadful! What happened to the Reverend Kenneth Barrington?'

'Out first ball, I'm afraid.'

'Who is doing all the damage then?'

'A bowler they've got called Father Trueman!'

Barry Johnston:

During a match between St Peters and Horsted Keynes in May 1999, Sussex dentist Rob Hemingway sent an impressive six soaring over the boundary rope and into the car park, but the smile froze on his face when he heard the distinctive tinkle of broken glass. Hemingway had become the first batsman of the season to hit a six through his own car windscreen. 'It was quite nice to connect with the ball so early in the season,' said the unlucky dentist later, 'but then I heard the crack and thought, oops, whose car is that?'

Brian Johnston:

Harold Larwood was once staying with a friend in the West Country, and visited a village cricket match on the Saturday afternoon. The visiting side were one short and Larwood was pressed to play without anyone knowing who he was. As both umpires came from the home side, who were batting, it proved difficult to get them out.

In desperation, the captain asked Larwood if he could bowl. He said that he would have a try and, taking a short run, sent down an off-spinner, which the batsman missed. It hit him in the middle of both legs, which were right in front of the wicket. Larwood appealed and 'Not out' was the reply. The next one, a leg-break, was snicked into the wicket-keeper's hands. Again 'Not out' was the reply.

Larwood then took his usual run of over twenty yards and sent down a thunderbolt, which knocked all three stumps out of the ground. Turning to the umpire he said, 'We very nearly had him that time, didn't we?'

COMMENTATORS

Brian Johnston:

The great thing is we do have fun in the commentary box, and we hope we communicate that fun through the microphone. You can't do this without wonderful people in the box and one of them was the great E.W. 'Jim' Swanton. Jim was a marvellous commentator on both radio and television and a great summariser, on television especially. He also wrote for years for *The Cricketer* and the *Daily Telegraph*.

He used to play the odd round of golf, and his ambition was to be a Second World War golfer – out in thirty-nine, back in forty-five!

On tours, though, he was a bit pompous. He used to stay with Governor Generals and arrive at the ground with a flag on the car! In fact, when he was on *Desert Island Discs*, Roy Plomley said, 'Mr Swanton, how do you think you would cope with being on a desert island?'

Jim said, 'It depends who the Governor General was!'

He's a great talker, and I rang up his wife the other day and said, 'How's Jim?'

She said, 'I haven't spoken to him for about three and a half days.'

'Really,' I said, 'has he been away?'

'No,' she said, 'I didn't like to interrupt!'

Jim was always very keen on the differential between the amateur and the professional. He thought it was a good thing. But I think he carried it a bit far when he refused to drive in the same car as his chauffeur!

Richie Benaud:

There are times when, sitting back in your living-rooms, you might think from the slight rise in tone in the commentator's voice that he is excited or, without you knowing it, it could be that a little glitch has appeared. It might be that a camera has 'gone' just at a crucial moment, something to do with sound, or someone may have pressed an unusual button somewhere in the world.

It might be something to do with the commentator, it could be something to do with production in the director's van at the ground and, on the rare occasion the latter might occur, I have been known to say softly into the 'lazy' mike, 'Everything all right down there . . . ?'

Just after the England v New Zealand Test at Old Trafford in 1994 we went to Headingley to cover the NatWest match between Yorkshire and Somerset. Due to the rain, the commentators' roster turned into a dog's

breakfast with additions, deletions and initials everywhere, and Tony Lewis, as presenter, was doing a brilliant
job of providing interviews, detail and all other things
necessary when nothing at all is happening on the field.

Coming up to what would have been teatime, I knew
that I, in the commentary box, needed to keep an eye
on things for Jack Bannister, who was on air in the studio
with Tony and Geoff Boycott. But, for some reason, I
put my brain into Plan B mode and settled down at the
small table, earpiece in my ear listening to the discussion,
and started on a sandwich and a cup of tea.

I was able to hear the interesting chat between Tony,
Jack and Geoff and see it on the monitor on the table
beside me. Suddenly there was a frenzied shout from the
van and in my ear because Tony had said, 'And now to
Richie Benaud in the commentary box.' Plan B changed
to Plan A in an instant. I moved at considerable speed
and with mixed success.

I dropped the sandwich on the floor and banged my
right knee hard on the side of the chair. With the pain
from that, I dropped my binoculars on the chair, and
my earpiece, which was connecting me with the shouts
from the van, became entangled in the connecting wires.
When I joined it all together, I found the plug was out
of, instead of in, the sound box.

Eventually, while everyone else was hysterically helpless, I was able to say in a suitably calm voice, with only

a slight edge to it, 'Now that you've had time to study the scorecard at your leisure . . . !'

In my ear there came an equally calm Welsh voice, but with a definite hint of laughter about it, as Tony Lewis inquired, 'Everything all right up there . . . ?'

Bill Frindall:

John Arlott was certainly the easiest commentator to work with. He rarely required me to pass him anything except the bowling figures or another bottle. He did startle me once during an Ashes Test but it was after he had lunched well.

He said, 'What I really want to know, Bill, is if England bowl their overs at the same rate as Australia did, and Brearley and Boycott survive the opening spell, and there are not more than ten no-balls in the innings, and assuming that my car does 33.8 miles per gallon and my home is 67.3 miles from here, what time does my wife have to put the casserole in?'

Brian Johnston:

At Port of Spain during Colin Cowdrey's successful MCC tour in 1967, I played a dirty trick on the West Indian commentator Tony Cozier. Rain had stopped play and he had gone across to the press box on the other side of the ground. I stayed in the box to give an occasional up-to-date report on the weather. I saw Tony returning after a time, so as he entered the box I pretended that we were on the air, and that I was broadcasting.

'Well,' I began, 'those were the statistics of the MCC team with their exact batting and bowling figures, plus their ages and dates of their birthdays. Thank you, Bearders. Ah, I see that Tony Cozier has just rejoined us, so I will ask him to give exactly the same details of the whole West Indian side. Tony . . .'

I have rarely seen a greater look of horror on anyone's face. He sat down at the mike and began to stammer, making frantic signals to our scorer to hand him *Wisden* or any other book that would give him the necessary information.

'Well, Brian,' he said, 'I'll try to tell the listeners in a minute, but as I've just seen the pitch perhaps you would like to hear about its state first.'

'No, sorry, Tony,' I said, 'we've just talked about it while you were away. All we want – and straight away please – is the information about the West Indian statistics.'

At this point I couldn't go on any further, he looked so miserable and desperate, so I said, 'Well, if Tony won't give us the details, I suppose we had better return to the studio. So goodbye from us all here.' There was a deathly hush for a few seconds, broken only by Tony

Cozier's heavy breathing. Then I said, 'Well done, boys. Very good rehearsal!'

It took Tony about five minutes to recover.

Richie Benaud:

When Channel 4 took over from the BBC in 1999 there was no doubt about the change in television coverage. Like the BBC, Channel 4 went to horseracing on occasions during the afternoon on a Saturday or holiday, but it was very rare for them to go to a news bulletin, which in the late 1990s had become part of the BBC's standard cricket telecast. The newsreaders were very good but Tony Lewis had a moment he would like to forget in the handover to one of them, the experienced Moira Stuart.

Tony was one of the best television presenters and commentators with whom I've ever worked. We agreed that a day's commentary was like a day playing Test cricket – one must have energy, a clear mind, a solid performance, concentration and quality throughout the day, always with your brain in gear before moving your lips.

Tony, known by some as 'AR', tells against himself the story of when, in the late 1990s, he and Geoff Boycott were on the roof at the Edgbaston ground doing a chat show concerning 'Best Catches' and 'Viewers'

Questions and Answers'. Keith Mackenzie was directing and the instructions were that at the end of the session, Tony was to hand back to Moira Stuart at Broadcasting House. The handover had to be perfectly timed.

One problem I could visualise from the commentary box was that the positioning of the monitors on the roof was such that the blazing sunshine was making it close to impossible to see what was on the screen. Tony said later that 'close to impossible' was well short of the mark, it was *totally* impossible. He filled exactly the twenty seconds required, threw to Moira Stuart, in his ear was given the all clear and assumed that to be correct.

Never has the phrase 'assume nothing' been more pertinent because the correct cut-off switch had *not* been pressed in the van, or in London, or possibly both. That was why AR's *'For f***'s sake'* made it to Moira at the news desk and to a few hundred thousand living-rooms around the country, also to the office desk of Jonathan Martin, BBC's Head of Sport.

After lunch AR read out a prepared apology and also apologised to the head man of the BBC. He needed a bit of lightening up, which was provided a few hours later when Ian Chappell sent him a message which read simply, 'Congratulations AR, mate, one-all.'

This was a reminder to the effect that Ian had previously made a similar error, having been told he was 'off-air' when in fact the wrong switch had been pressed and he was still 'on-air'.

It wasn't long before Chappell had taken a 2–1 lead in the 'assume nothing' stakes!

Bill Frindall:

Trevor Bailey could be splendidly vague and absent-minded at times. On the rest day of his debut Test in 1949 against New Zealand at Headingley, he took his wife on an unsuccessful trip to find the seaside at the spa town of Harrogate. On one memorable occasion, he entered the commentary box, rubbed his hands with glee and announced that he had just bought a new car.

'What did you buy?' I asked.

He replied, 'I'm not sure. It's a blue one!'

Michael Atherton:

On my first day for Channel 4 at Lord's I made sure I sat in the box whenever Richie Benaud was commentating. During the afternoon Michael Slater was on air and was all of a muddle. He wanted to use the past tense of the word 'sneak' but wasn't sure whether it should be 'snuck' or 'sneaked'. He turned to the doyen of commentators, who was eating a sandwich and studying the form.

'Hey, Rich,' he whispered, 'can I use the word snuck, or is it sneaked? Whadya think?'

Richie finished his sandwich and then ticked his fancy. Then, in characteristic fashion, he raised an eyebrow and half turned to Slater.

'Michael,' he said, 'quite a few "ucks" spring to mind but "sn" is not one of them!'

Brian Johnston:

We used to pull Jim Swanton's leg unmercifully. One famous example happened in 1963 during that wonderful Test match against the West Indies at Lord's, when Colin Cowdrey came in at number eleven, his wrist in plaster, two balls to go and six runs to win, and with David Allen at the other end. It was a draw, but it was a great match.

Before it started, Jim and I were doing the television and we were told, 'There's ten thousand people in St Peter's Square, waiting for that white puff of smoke to come out of the Vatican chimney and announce that a new Pope has been elected. If this happens during the Test, we'll leave it immediately and go over to our man in Rome, who'll tell us who the new Pope is.'

So we were waiting for this call to Rome, yapping away, doing the commentary, when out of the corner of

my eye I saw that the chimney on the Old Tavern had caught fire. Black smoke was belching out, so we got the cameras on to it and I said, 'There you are. Jim Swanton's been elected Pope!'

Min Patel:

You would think Michael Holding would know his way around the UK, having spent numerous summers on the county circuit with Derbyshire, then later as a television pundit. But when he was commentating on the Fourth West Indies v England Test at Old Trafford in 1995, he was still unsure how to negotiate the approximately two-mile drive from the Copthorne Hotel in Salford Quays to the ground.

Then Mikey had a moment of pure genius. He would follow one of the England team (who were also in residence there) to the ground. Spotting a certain G.A. Hick heading out of the front doors, Michael sped to his car.

It was about an hour later, while heading south down the M6 at a fair lick, that it dawned on the Windies speedster that Hick had been left out of the final eleven and was heading home to Worcester!

Henry Blofeld:

Rex Alston was another great commentator. He died in 1994, at the age of ninety-three, but he was an extraordinary chap. He was a schoolmaster by trade, and they always say about schoolmasters, 'a man among boys, a boy among men'. There was a little bit of that about Rex. He was naïve. I don't think he'd ever really visited the fleshpots of life, although that may be unkind. But the most extraordinary thing once happened to him.

Towards the end of his life, in 1985, he came up to a dinner in London. He was staying at the East India and Sports Club, I suppose because he was a sportsman – he certainly wasn't East Indian! – but he was taken ill in the middle of the night and rushed off to the Westminster Hospital. The next morning the matron came in, holding a copy of *The Times*, and said, 'Good morning, Mr Alston, I've come to read you your obituary.' His obituary was in the paper!

John Woodcock, the cricket journalist, had written it – for the elderly, the obituaries are usually written in advance and he'd been asked to do one about Rex, knowing that he was getting on a bit. So Woodcock had written it and sent it in to *The Times*. It was a busy day at the paper and the obituaries editor had seen it and thought, 'Oh dear, poor old Rex.' He'd put it in his out-tray and it appeared in the paper the next day.

I rang up John Woodcock because we'd had a party for the BBC at the Lord's Banqueting Suite earlier in the week, when Rex had been in absolutely mid-season form, and I said to Johnny, 'It's awfully sad.'

He said, 'Blowers, you're the second person who's rung me this morning. You'll be very surprised to hear who the first caller was!'

When he told me, I asked him, 'What did you say to Rex?'

Johnny said, 'The first thing I said to him was, "Rex, now tell me, *where* exactly are you calling from?"'

Brian Johnston:

I wish I could tell you all Fred Trueman's one liners, but they're not quite suitable. He told me a clean one last year. He said, 'Johnners, hear about the Pole who went to have his eyes tested? The oculist said, "Can you read that bottom line on the chart?" The Pole said, "Read it? He's my best friend!"'

I think I can risk this one because it's very funny. About a year ago he said, 'Johnners? Hear about the flasher who was about to retire?'

I said, 'No, Fred, I haven't.'

'Oh,' he said, 'he's decided to stick it out for another year!'

Barry Johnston:

Jim Swanton and Brian Johnston were the guest speakers at the Cricketer Cup dinner in 1986 at the Café Royal in London. Swanton spoke first, and at the end of his speech he gave an outrageous plug for his new book, *Barclays World of Cricket: The Game from A-Z*. 'It's a marvellous book,' declared Swanton, pompously, 'required reading by every student of the game, and it is very good value at only eighteen pounds fifty in all good bookshops.'

Brian was up next. 'I must say I agree with Jim, for once,' he said. 'His book is excellent value for money. When you consider that a new cricket ball costs twenty pounds, if you buy his book you can get a whole load of balls for just eighteen pounds fifty!'

Henry Blofeld:

I got on very well with John Arlott, but he wasn't an easy man. He was a legend in his own lunchtime – he had an absolutely unquenchable thirst and he was a prodigious drinker of claret. My definitive Arlott story happened at the first Test match I was lucky enough to commentate on at Lord's.

On the second day of the Lord's Test match in those days, the Director General of the BBC, in his infinite wisdom, always had a private dinner party for the members of *Test Match Special*. Now that was frightfully chuffing and all the rest of it, but actually it was a bloody nuisance, because Broadcasting House was at the other end of London from where I lived, and I had to rush back home and change. It was desperately difficult to get there on time and I just breasted the tape at about 8.27.

I knew it was going to be a bad evening when the Director General was in the act of throwing the keys of the drink cupboard to Trevor Bailey with the words, 'Lock up when there's nothing left!' I don't know how well you know Trevor Bailey, but when I tell you that he didn't go to bed until he was fifty-three you'll know what I mean!

Anyway, at about two o'clock we were down to warm water and so we legged it home. Being a new boy, I got to Lord's quite early the next morning, at about nine-thirty. If you don't know the Lord's pavilion, you go in the back entrance, and then you go up half a flight of stairs to the first landing, which is the Long Room level. There are these rubberised stairs with pockmarks from cricketers' boots, and it smells like a cross between linseed oil and stale jockstraps, the sort of thing that sets cricketers' noses a-twitching about March and April.

I'd got up to the first landing and was contemplating ascending the next three staircases to the commentary box at the top, when I heard a noise like a broken oak tree behind me. 'Henry, will you give me a hand with these?' and there was the great man, Arlott, sweating profusely, mopping his brow with a red-spotted handkerchief, with two enormous brown briefcases.

I rushed downstairs and said, 'Of course,' and picked one up, which was very heavy. I thought of *Wisden*s and other learned tomes, and I picked up the other, which was almost as heavy, and I thought of more *Wisden*s and more learned tomes. We got back to the Long Room level, when the great man spoke again. 'Henry,' he said, 'before we climb Everest we'll go and pay Maisie a visit.'

The Long Room bar, which is parallel and behind the Long Room, was in those days presided over by a lady of Irish extraction called Maisie. Maisie had nothing much going for her except for one thing – she had pink hair. Now pink hair is quite unusual, but the thing about her hair was that it was never the same two days running. Some days it was shocking pink, other days it was not quite so shocking, and then it was more shocking than you could ever believe. I think this was a fairly modest day and we went into the Long Room bar, which had just opened, and Arlott spoke again.

'Maisie,' he said, 'we'll have two quadruple brandies.'

I said, 'No. No, John, not after last night. I'll have some black coffee.'

'Maisie,' he said, 'we'll still have the two quadruples.'

I kid you not, he had a Force Nine hangover on the Richter scale and it was only by dint of getting both hands together and pulling in opposite directions that he eventually got the drink down; some of it went here and there, but quite a lot of it went in. It steadied him up and, to show off, he picked the next one up rather shakily in his left hand and threw it back, got almost all of it in the right place, and I thought, 'Thank goodness for that, now we can get on with the day's work.' Not a bit of it!

'Maisie,' he said, 'to complete the cure, we'll have a third quadruple,' which came and went with sickening speed. There we were at about twenty minutes to ten and the old boy had downed half a bottle of brandy!

We set off up the three flights of stairs. He went at the double and I staggered behind with these great heavy briefcases and I put them down on the green baize table in the corner of the commentary box. I can remember Johnners was there in his co-respondent brown-and-white shoes, Christopher Martin-Jenkins was there and our producer, Peter Baxter – I think they'd been recording a programme. When I'd put the cases down, Arlott waited for a moment and then advanced upon the table with the sort of smile on his face that I can only think the Duke of Wellington would have worn when he left Waterloo for the last time. It was a little bit self-satisfied, I'm bound to say, and pleased.

He went and opened the first briefcase and took out six bottles of claret. He opened the second briefcase and took out four bottles of claret, one or two glasses, corkscrews and sundry bits and pieces, and then he turned to the box. We were all absolutely open-mouthed and he made the immortal remark, 'Well, with any good fortune, that little lot should see us through until the lunch interval!'

BOWLERS

Dickie Bird:

I would like to have seen Harold Larwood and Bill Voce bowl. They both played for Nottinghamshire and England and I'm told they were very, very quick. One time they were playing Northamptonshire at Northampton and in those days they had a fast bowler in the Northampton-shire side called Nobby Clark. He was very fast. He was left-arm over the wicket and he was letting the Nottinghamshire batsmen have everything – bouncers, beamers, the lot. They were ducking all over the place. The Northamptonshire lads said, 'Hey, Nobby, don't you think you ought to bowl them a few half-volleys? We've got to go in to bat and they've got Larwood and Voce, two of the world's fastest bowlers.'

'What're you frightened of?' said Nobby. 'I'm not frightened of Larwood and Voce. When I come in to bat, if Larwood pitches it in my half I shall hit him straight back over his head. If Larwood bowls short, I'll hook him straight out of Northampton. What're you frightened of?'

Nobby had got seven wickets and Larwood came in at number nine. The first ball to Larwood, Nobby let him have a vicious bouncer, straight at his head. Larwood just got out of the way of it. He said, 'Nobby, it will soon be my turn.'

Nobby said, 'Yes, and I shall be ready for you. When I come in to bat for Northamptonshire, you pitch them in my half, Lol, and I'm going to hit you straight back over your head. You bowl them short and I'm going to hook you straight out of Northampton.'

Larwood said, 'It will be a good contest.'

Northamptonshire went in to bat and they tell me they've never seen bowling as quick as they saw that day from Larwood and Voce. They just ran through them, and Nobby came out to bat at number nine. As he was taking guard off the umpire, Lol Larwood said, 'Now then, Nobby, it's *my* turn.'

Nobby said, 'Yes, and I'm ready for you. You pitch them in my half, I'm going to hit you straight back over your head. You bowl them short and I'm going to hook you straight out of Northampton.'

Larwood said, 'We'll see about that.'

In came Larwood, first ball to Nobby, and he bowled him a vicious bouncer, straight at Nobby's head. Nobby didn't just sway out of the way of it, he jumped out of the way, and as the ball went past he flashed at it. Nobby got a thick edge and the ball flew to third slip, who caught it *after* it had bounced two yards in front of him.

Everybody looked up. Nobby, bat under his arm, gloves off, was walking back to the pavilion.

'Come back and fight!' said Larwood. 'Come back and fight!'

'Oh, well bowled, Lol,' said Nobby. 'Well bowled.'

The umpire said, 'Come back, Mr Clark! He didn't catch it. It bounced two yards in front of third slip before he caught it.'

But Nobby kept on walking. He said, 'I am satisfied it was a fair catch, Mr Umpire . . . !'

Andrew Strauss:

Darren Gough was the life and soul of the England team for more than a decade and after a couple of days in his company it was easy to see why. He has an enormous amount of confidence in his ability and he never appears to let things get him down. England might be struggling and Gough may have been smashed around the park, yet he is still full of optimism and enthusiasm. One famous Gough story comes from the 1998/99 tour of Australia when England's bowlers were getting hit all around the Bellerive Oval in Hobart.

The game was in mid-December and Gough, who was not playing in the match, thought it would be funny to come in at the tea interval dressed as Santa Claus and hand out presents. The dressing room would have been a pretty glum place as Gough walked in and everyone was wondering what he would do next.

He chuckled, 'Ho! Ho! Ho! Gussy and Corky. No wonder this bag feels so heavy – it's got your bowling figures in it!'

The batsmen rolled about the dressing room in laughter. The bowlers wanted to strangle him.

Dickie Bird:

During the days of Wilfred Rhodes, one of the greatest all-round cricketers the world has ever seen, Yorkshire paid a visit to Cambridge University and the Yorkshire and England legend was bowling to a young University freshman. To the amazement of everyone, the batsman proceeded to knock Rhodes all over the field and went in at lunch on 99 not out.

While they were having lunch, one of the Cambridge players said to the batsman, 'I can't believe what you've just done. You do know, don't you, who it is that you've just been thrashing around Fenners?'

The young man replied, 'No, I've no idea. Who is it?'

'That,' said his team-mate, 'just happens to be the great Wilfred Rhodes.'

The batsman was still reeling from that piece of

information when he resumed his innings at the start of the afternoon session, needing just one more for his century. Now knowing who the bowler was, he was a bag of nerves – and was out first ball!

Ian Brayshaw:

When Australian fast bowler Dennis Lillee was at his peak in the early and middle 1970s, his sheer speed was enough to put a falter in the step of the best batsmen in the world. As the years passed he naturally slowed down a little but he retained the ability to throw in the occasional scorcher, just to let them know it was still there. Umpire Robin Bailhache tells the story of Lillee toiling away with little help from a pretty flat wicket in the First Test against the West Indies at the Brisbane Cricket Ground in 1979/80.

It was hot, frustrating toil for a bowler of Lillee's type and after a while the champion became a little worn and exasperated. At the end of one over a dejected Lillee

stood halfway down the pitch and Bailhache moved to save him the walk back to get his hat. As he handed it over, a rather haggard-looking Lillee said:

'Jeez, it's hard being a fast bowler and I ought to know . . . I used to be one!'

Dickie Bird:

The Sussex and England fast bowler John Snow was involved in a memorable prank in a county championship game at Leicester. It was cold and it was raining on and off, although not heavily enough to justify abandoning the game. The spectators gradually drifted away so that eventually the only people left watching were the scorers and officials.

After yet another stoppage Snow went out to resume his over. He took out of his pocket a bright red soap cricket ball that he had bought at the local Woolworths, and craftily swapped it for the real thing. His first delivery was the perfect bouncer. The soap ball skidded on the damp grass and Peter Marner, the Leicestershire bats-man, got into position for a fierce hook, which he completed with impeccable timing. The ball shattered into fragments.

The Sussex scorer, Len Chandler, placed an asterisk beside the dot in his book, and at the bottom of the page, he elaborated briefly, 'Ball exploded!'

Brian Johnston:

Arthur Mailey, the great Australian leg-spinner, was bowling for New South Wales in a famous match in which Victoria scored 1,107 against them. Mailey's figures were 4 for 362. Afterwards he said, 'I should have had an even better analysis if a bloke in a brown trilby hat sitting in the sixth row of the pavilion roof hadn't dropped two sitters!'

Henry Blofeld:

Arthur Mailey's Test career ended when the stuffy Australian authorities kicked him out of the game for writing about it while he was still playing. As well as writing about cricket, he also had a short spell as a general news reporter. One day Mailey was sent by his editor to cover the funeral of an ex-Lord Mayor of Melbourne. Mailey's story was weighty enough to satisfy the most gloom-laden witness of the sad occasion, but even so his editor sent for him more in anger than in sorrow.

'Do you know how many names you've mentioned?' demanded the editor. 'Three hundred and eighteen. You've got three hundred and seventeen right. The one you've got wrong is the name of the corpse!'

Barry Johnston:

Dennis Lillee was bowling to a batsman who kept playing and missing. After a while the Australian fast bowler could stand it no longer. Lillee went up to the batsman and said, 'I know why you're batting so badly.'

Naturally curious, the batsman asked him why.

Lillee replied, 'Because you've got some shit on the end of your bat.'

The batsman picked up his bat and examined the end of it.

'Wrong end, mate,' said Lillee.

Dickie Bird:

During their 1966 tour of England, the West Indian officials became fed up with the practical jokes being played by members of their team and decided to put an end to them. Larking about was fine in small doses, but the players had gone too far, and enough was enough. Their manager, Jeffrey Stollmeyer, called all the players together to thrash out the matter in a team meeting.

Fast bowler Charlie Griffith arrived late and so didn't know what on earth they were talking about as he sat down to listen to the debate, but his ears pricked up when he heard Garry Sobers say, 'That's it, then. There has been far too much leg-pulling, and it has got to stop.'

Charlie was most indignant. 'No more leg-pulling?' he exclaimed. 'So how am I going to get any runs? That's the only shot I've got!'

Brian Johnston:

Leicestershire were playing Nottinghamshire and Harold Larwood was bowling at his fastest and was in his most frightening mood. The light was very bad and he had taken four quick wickets when it was Alec Skelding's turn to bat.

Skelding came down the pavilion steps very slowly. Then he groped his way along the railings in front of the pavilion, shouting to the members, 'Can anyone tell me where this match is being played . . . ?'

Andrew Strauss:

Darren Gough is always great value because of the stupid comments he comes out with. A journalist once asked him why he was nicknamed 'Rhino'.

'It's because I'm as strong as a bloody ox, that's why,' came the no-nonsense reply.

One morning Gough walked into the England

dressing room and informed the team that he had found a great new bar in town. It was lively and, apparently, it served excellent food. When asked what it was called, he replied in his best Barnsley/Italian accent, 'Albarone'.

Albarone? The room went quiet. It was only when he explained where the bar was that a colleague politely pointed out the place was actually called 'All Bar One'!

Michael Parkinson:

Cec Pepper spent most of his career in English league cricket but there was never any doubt about his roots. He was a dinky-di Aussie, a turbulent man and one of the best all-round cricketers Australia has ever produced. Pepper became one of the legendary figures in league cricket in the north of England. He was playing in one match at Burnley when an amateur in the side, Derek Chadwick, ran round the boundary to catch a skier off the Australian's bowling and collided with the sightscreen.

Play was held up while Mr Chadwick was revived, giving Mr Pepper time to mull over what he considered to be a chance missed off his bowling. Some time later, with Burnley struggling, the captain asked Pepper what he should do.

Cec replied, 'Why don't you get that lad to run into the sightscreen again, it might distract the batsmen!'

Fred Trueman:

The West Indian fast bowler Joel Garner once guested in a Sunday charity match in Surrey. During the tea interval he joined the queue for a plate of sandwiches as prepared by the club's tea ladies. On seeing him, one lady enthusiastically remarked, 'Oh my, you're a tall fellow, aren't you?'

When asked how tall he was, Joel replied, 'Six feet eight, ma'am.'

'Oooh,' cooed the tea lady, nudging her colleague, 'and are you all in proportion?'

'No, ma'am,' replied Joel. 'If I was, I'd be eleven feet six!'

Dickie Bird:

Merv Hughes was a tremendous character and I always got on well with him. But in a Test match at Headingley, England were playing Australia and Merv was bowling to Graeme Hick. Now Merv didn't rate Graeme Hick at all, he didn't think he could play, and his language was disgraceful. Honestly, Hick was playing and missing and Merv was swearing, with that big walrus moustache of his quivering, and I've never heard language like it.

I said, 'Merv, I want you to be a good boy. I want you to stop swearing.'

He said, 'This feller can't play.'

I said, 'Look, Merv, be a good boy and stop swearing, please. Now go back to your mark and get on with your bowling.'

Merv walked past me to go back to his mark, to bowl the next delivery, and he looked at me as he walked past. He said, 'Dickie, you're a legend!'

I said, 'Well, be a good boy now, no more swearing.'

He said, 'All right, Dickie, for you I'll not swear again.'

And next ball Hick played and missed and you've never heard language like it!

Barry Johnston:

In May 2003 Darren Gough made a cartoon cameo appearance in the children's comic *The Beano*. In a story featuring the character Billy Whizz, the England fast bowler was pictured alongside long-distance runner Paula Radcliffe, but was given only one word to say: 'Chortle!'

Brian Johnston:

After suffering from a surfeit of dropped catches in the slips off his bowling, the Surrey fast bowler Alf Gover was having a drink with some of the offenders after close of play. After a while one of them said, 'Well, so long Alf, I must be off. I've got a train to catch.'

Alf replied, 'So long. Hope you have better luck – with the train!'

Henry Blofeld:

I first saw Alec Bedser bowl in 1948, when he got Don Bradman out twice in his last Test match at Lord's. He went on to be an England selector and he was chairman of the selectors during the 1970s, but he didn't enjoy the new-fangled cricket. I suppose that's only natural. It was a very different game from the one he'd played.

Alec told me a lovely story about when he was chairman of the selectors. It was in 1975, the year of the first World Cup, when the Australians stayed on and played four Test matches. Alec didn't go near the dressing room during the game, but after every day's play he used to go in and talk to the captain, Tony Greig. They'd have a bit of a chat about tactics and what they were going to do the next day.

After the second day's play at The Oval in the Fourth Test, Alec went in to see Greig and while they were chatting, Alec heard this extraordinary whirring noise behind him. He said to Greig, 'Captain, what's that whirring noise?'

Greig looked over his shoulder and replied, 'Oh, that's Bob Woolmer's hairdryer.'

Alec said, 'Hairdryer? Hairdryer! What's wrong with a bleedin' towel?'

Dickie Bird:

I played with one of the greatest characters at Yorkshire – Fred Trueman. He was also a great fast bowler, although I thought Dennis Lillee of Australia was the best fast bowler I had ever seen, and I used to argue the point with Fred every time I saw him. He'd say, 'Tha' what? Huh! I can still bowl better now off five paces than he ever could!'

Fred was great fun to be with in the dressing room. We always had a laugh. Before a county championship match started, we'd get changed in the Yorkshire dressing room but Fred was never in our room before the match started. He always went to see the visitors. He didn't knock on the visitors' dressing-room door, he just used to smash it open.

He used to stand in the entrance and he'd say, 'Nah then lads, I'm here and I'm ready for you today. I can see you shaking a little bit, yes, you're looking a little bit uneasy. I think I might have eight or nine wickets here today. Oh, there's my old friend from last season. He was by the square-leg umpire when I bowled him. That's one wicket I've got for a start! Anyway, good luck, lads. I shall be ready for you in the middle. I can see all of you are looking a bit worried.'

If we'd lost the toss and the visitors were batting, the Yorkshire team would be out in the middle with the two umpires and we'd look around saying, 'Where's Fred?' And Freddie would be standing by the pavilion gates. He used to wait for the opposition opening batsmen, and as they came out through the gates he would say to them, 'Don't close that gate. You won't be long out here!'

Barry Johnston:

During the 2002/03 Ashes series in Australia, there was some discussion in the international media about the bowling action of the Australian fast bowler Brett Lee, suggesting it might not be entirely legal. At the Fourth Test in Melbourne the English touring supporters, 'The Barmy Army', were in full voice and they lost no opportunity to remind Lee that they considered him to be a chucker. Whenever the young Australian came in to bowl, the English fans would call out, 'No-ball!' causing the Australian batsman Justin Langer to label them 'a disgrace'.

When Brett Lee was not bowling, he fielded directly in front of the English fans and it seems he took their good-natured stick in his stride. At one point he even responded with a smile when the Barmy Army asked him for a wave. The smile was soon wiped off his face, however, when they asked him to repeat the gesture . . . but with a straight arm!

Michael Parkinson:

When he was in his eighties, the Australian bowling legend Bill 'Tiger' O'Reilly had to have one of his legs amputated below the knee. Neither cruel illness nor old age could change his feisty manner. He was a mettlesome man, full of opinion and argument.

When I called to inquire about his condition, he said, 'I just sit here watching the kitchen wall in case someone runs off with it. It is a very boring occupation but I have to tell you that it is infinitely more interesting than watching one-day cricket!'

Michael Atherton:

It was my final Test match. Australia had progressed serenely to 641 for 4 and had enforced the follow-on. On the Sunday evening I had played my last innings and now, as the team went out to prepare for the final day, I stayed in the dressing room at The Oval for treatment. It was almost as if I was physically removing myself now that my contribution was done. I looked upon the match situation, and the problems, dispassionately, from a distance.

I was determined to enjoy my last day, however. Mostly, I watched on television from a corner in the dressing room, trying to commit to memory a place I might never see again.

In the afternoon Graham Thorpe hobbled in. 'I'm sorry to have missed your last game, Athers,' he said, 'but I'm proud to have played with you.' At the end, Duncan Fletcher, the England coach, gave a small speech of thanks for my efforts over the last fifteen years, and urged everyone to come to the dinner in my honour that night. I was getting a little emotional. I wasn't the only one. Phil Tufnell had taken a mauling in the match. Now he sauntered over with a fag in his mouth and a sad look on his face. I took his limp, outstretched hand and awaited his eulogy.

'Athers,' he said, 'I bowled all right, didn't I? Jesus, I've gone for a hundred and seventy on a "bunsen" but I bowled well . . . didn't I?'

Brian Johnston:

There are so many stories about Fred Trueman, but one, which Norman Yardley assured me is true, occurred in about 1949, when Fred was eighteen or so. In those days Yorkshire used to go and play matches against various clubs to get fit for the cricket season. Nowadays, people run ten times round the ground or do press-ups, but in those days they used to play cricket to get fit for cricket, which was good!

They were playing the Yorkshire Gentlemen at Escrick and Fred, very young, virile and tough, bowled very fast bouncers at these poor Yorkshire Gentlemen. Four of them were carried off and went to hospital. They were about 26 for 6 when out of the pavilion came a figure with grey hair, white bristling moustache, I Zingari cap with a button, and a silk shirt buttoned up at the sleeves.

Norman went up to Fred and said, 'Look, this is Brigadier So-and-So, patron of the club. Treat him gently, Fred.' So Fred, who was a generous man, went up to the apprehensive-looking Brigadier and, with a lovely smile, said, 'Don't worry, Brigadier. Don't worry. I'll give you one to get off the mark.'

The Brigadier's face relaxed in a smile, only to freeze with horror as Fred said, 'Aye, and with second I'll pin you against flippin' sightscreen!'

Dickie Bird:

Fred Trueman made his mark in his first Test series in 1952 when the Indians visited Headingley. He destroyed their batting with some fearsome fast bowling, and at one time the visitors had four men back in the pavilion without a single run having been scored in their second innings as Freddie set about them.

Twenty-two years later, the manager of the 1974 touring party was Lieutenant Colonel Hemu Adhikari, who had been one of Fred's victims that day. They met in the bar at Old Trafford during a Test there, and Fred put out his hand and said, 'Hello, Colonel, I'm pleased to see you've got your colour back!'

Barry Johnston:

When Dennis Lillee and Jeff Thomson were at the height of their fame they were interviewed together on Australian television. At one point the interviewer asked Lillee, 'Tell me, Dennis, what would you do if you discovered you had only thirty minutes to live?'

Lillee replied, 'I'd make love to the first thing that moved!'

The interviewer turned to Thomson, 'And what would you do, Jeff?'

Thommo replied, 'I wouldn't move for half an hour!'

Henry Blofeld:

There's a nice story about dear old Alan Ross, who wrote beautifully for the *Observer* on cricket for about twenty or thirty years and was editor of the *London Magazine*.

Alan had his finest hour during a game of cricket at Lord's in 1969. The New Zealand cricket side were over here that year and they had in their ranks a chap called Bob Cunis, who wasn't quite a fast bowler, and wasn't quite a slow bowler, and wasn't quite a medium-pace bowler. Alan wrote this one Sunday in the *Observer* and

I have a cutting at home: 'The problem with Cunis is that his bowling is rather like his name. It's neither one thing nor the other!'

Dickie Bird:

Although small of stature, Alfred 'Tich' Freeman, of Kent and England, was another giant of the past. Between the wars he claimed 3,776 wickets – a total bettered only by the great Wilfred Rhodes – and he was the only player to take more than 300 wickets in a season.

When 'Tich' retired from county cricket he christened his house, 'Dunbowlin'. His wife was reputedly a bit of a dragon, and the story goes that when Freeman's funeral cortège was late arriving at the church one friend was heard to whisper, 'She probably hasn't let him come!'

OVERSEAS TOURS

Brian Johnston:

I went to India for the first time in 1993 to commentate on England's Test matches in Madras and Bombay. It is a very strange country. In fact, I still don't know whether they drive on the left or the right. They steer very well, even around the cows lying in the middle of the road, but it is all very frightening.

And, of course, the food is very tricky, but they have got a new dish especially for Englishmen. It's called Boycott curry. You still get the runs, but more slowly!

David Lloyd:

After I retired from first-class cricket, I was asked to coach the England Under-19 team on their winter tours. Graham Saville, the former Essex batsman, was the manager, and excellent at the job. He was not a tranquil man to have about the place, though. In fact, he was on blood pressure pills as he tended to get over-excited rather easily.

Early in 1996, the Under-19s were on tour in Zimbabwe and we were staying at the Holiday Inn in Bulawayo. At 6 a.m. one day we were loading up the bus for the drive back to Harare, when the hotel manager made an appearance. He had a complaint. There were some unpaid bills, which is unacceptable on any tour.

'What names are on them?' demanded Graham Saville, with a warning flash of anger.

Without even a hint of a smile, the hotel manager replied, 'Mick Jagger, Cliff Richard and Prince Monolulu!'

Graeme Fowler:

It was the third day of the Third Test against India at Calcutta, January 1985. Boring Shastri, boring Azharuddin. Both got centuries, which seemed their main concern, but on the flattest, most placid wicket imaginable. We kept ourselves amused by fooling around. Our entertainments ranged from fielding in police hats, acrobatics, conducting the crowd's cries of 'We want Kapil', to throwing in rubber balls. Anything to make a dull day pass more quickly, but also to wake us up.

Then 151 overs into the match, our all-rounder, Chris Cowdrey, came on to bowl. He also provided the highlight of the day. After tea he had Mike Gatting at first slip. David Gower said, 'Do you want Gatt a foot wider?'

'No,' said Cowdrey, 'he'd burst!'

Henry Blofeld:

Michael Melford of the *Daily Telegraph* was a great character. He was always ill and I remember the first tour I ever did to India in 1963/64. Melford was staying at the Connemara Hotel in Madras, where the First Test match was being played. One morning he came down to breakfast and joined John Woodcock of *The Times* and myself. Mellers always looked like Banquo's ghost but he was even more like a ghost this particular morning. He looked absolutely white.

Wooders said, 'Mellers! Is it as bad as that?'

Mellers said, 'Jolly nearly.'

'What happened?'

'I had the most dreadful night.'

'How bad?'

'Well,' he said, 'I'll tell you how bad it was. I went to the loo twenty-one times. But I'm not claiming a world record, because I was wind-assisted!'

Dickie Bird:

One match I umpired in the West Indies during 1993 stands out in my memory. It was against Pakistan at the Antiguan Recreation Ground at St John's. During the Pakistan innings I was standing at square-leg, keeping a keen eye on the batsmen as they scampered for a quick single, when I felt an excruciating pain right at the base of my spine. I thought I'd been shot. The pain travelled all the way down my leg and I collapsed in agony.

It turned out that Keith Arthurton, one of the hardest throwers in world cricket, had hurled the ball in from a position just behind me and had made a slight error in the missile's intended flight path. The physio dashed on, had a quick look, and ordered, 'Right, Dickie, on your feet, and drop your trousers.'

I looked at him aghast. 'I can't do that. Not in front of all these people.'

'Please yourself,' came the brusque reply. 'But I'm warning you, if you don't let me spray the area, then you're going to end up in even more pain. The bruise will be so bad that you won't be able to walk. You'll have a very serious problem.'

There was, it seemed, nothing else for it. So I reluctantly unfastened my belt and allowed my trousers to fall to my ankles, revealing brightly coloured underpants and the Bird lunch-box in all their combined glory.

'Right-oh, then,' I told him, 'get on with it.' And in my most Methodist ministerial fashion, I added, 'Let us spray!'

Angus Bell: Batting on the Bosphorus

When I was a whippersnapper I always wanted to play international cricket. I dreamed of steaming in as a tearaway for England and uprooting Brian Lara's off stump. It was a sad day at school when, alas, fully grown at five foot eight, I had to ditch fast bowling and switch to gentle leg-spin. I realised I was never going to make it for England. Not deterred entirely, I lowered my sights, setting them on Scotland. It was even more pathetic the day I realised I wasn't going to cut the crust there either. Never in my youth in the Scottish hills, however, did I imagine I'd get my first international cap for Slovakia.

'All our games are internationals,' said Vladimir as we drove to the football field in his red Škoda. 'Tonight it's Slovakia A versus Slovakia B. You can be captain of the A-team, my friend.'

Captain. On debut. Of the A-team. My cheeks flushed and my chest swelled. It was a shame my parents couldn't be here to see this.

I asked Vladimir about the make-up of the squad. Seventy per cent were gardening and/or politics students, he said, and all were native. They also batted left-handed. 'I think this is because of ice hockey.'

But the most startling statistic leapt out from the Slovak team-sheet. Move over the Waugh brothers, Slovakia had four Juricek members, three other sets of brothers and two cousins.

'Their mothers are very proud,' said Vladimir.

The Slovaks arrived by rollerblade, bicycle and moped. Although most of the players had passed their English exams only a week ago, it was a struggle to get anything more than 'hello' out of them.

'These guys,' said Vladimir, pointing at two teammates, 'recently applied to Nitra University. Everyone must sit entrance exams, unless they are a member of a Slovak national sports team. Nitra University approved their applications based on them playing cricket. But, guess what. They have batting averages of two and zero. One of them has never scored a run in his life!'

The successful applicants giggled and nodded when they understood.

The plastic green pitch was wheeled out to the centre circle. Once Vladimir had broken up a minor scuffle between kids, the players gathered for the toss. In my first coin-flip as an international captain, nerves spoiled the occasion. The coin landed down my shirt. When it popped out, it showed heads and I'd lost. As so few players spoke English, I couldn't work out which team was batting and which was bowling. I didn't even know who was in which team.

It appeared my A-team was inserted first. The B medium pacers showed little mercy in their tracksuits, exploiting centre-circle demons to the full. The ball kicked and spat past our openers' heads, and in the follow-up deliveries promptly flattened their stumps. The bails landed in the hands of the old-fashioned backstop.

In a recovery job Kevin Pietersen's mum would have been proud of, our middle order plundered the short, square boundaries. Each four was cheered by players and spectators as though this was a World Cup final. Even the players' girlfriends had turned out to clap and do the scorebook.

At the end of an over I walked down the wicket to discuss tactics with my partner. 'Don't be afraid to pick up your bat and smack it,' I said. My partner stared back, not understanding a word. I realised I'd have to resign my captaincy forthwith. There was no way I'd be able to set fields in the second innings.

After Vladimir's tight mix of pace and spin, the B-team used paper-scissors-stone to decide who'd bowl their final overs. By the end of our allotted twenty, the As had accelerated to 97 for 5. Bearded truck-driver Stalin, one of the four Juricek brothers, had unselfishly guided me to my first international 50. Tired from his 0 not out, he then had to leave to paint his room orange. A substitute was sought from the stands.

At the innings change, a storm began to whip across the field. Entrusted with the new ball by the second captain – a rarity for a leg-spinner – I suffered a haunting flashback of my first school match. Back then we played in starched, white school shirts and cream, cotton shorts. We wore knee-high red socks, held up by garters, with combs tucked into their rims. School rules dictated hair *always* had to be side-parted. As former England managers will testify, this is what made a good cricketer. The wind in that first game caused my hair to fly all over the place. I lost my side parting and my radar. I bowled thirteen wides in a single over. It was a feat that saw me go from the Under-12s' opening paceman to scorer for the rest of the season. As I looked at Lubos facing me now, bent over at a right angle, I had a horrible feeling my international career could meet the same fate.

I approached the wicket and released. Lubos' leg stump was sent cartwheeling backwards. The poor lad had been up since four that morning for work.

Their favoured forward defensive prods à la French cricket couldn't save B's top three being fired out. And when they suffered two direct hit run-outs from the boundary in two balls – the second from a lazily jogged single – it all looked to be over.

But Vladimir, relishing his captain's role, looted the vacant leg-side boundary with sweeps. He gained admirable support from the player selected for university without ever having scored a run. He chose this opportunity to register his personal best. He scored 2, and received the loudest cheer of the day.

In a desperate move, we tried the same bowler from each end in succession. Even this illegal ploy couldn't stop a final stand of 40, and a loss by two wickets, with just one ball to spare.

As Vladimir was carried off the field for his winning 55, thirty villagers cheering, he turned to say, 'This was our greatest ever game!'

Barry Johnston:

During the England tour of New Zealand in early 2008, Ian Bell made a vital century in the final Test at Napier, but it was a comment from his girlfriend, Chantelle, that has gone down in cricket legend. Chantelle was invited along with the other England WAGS to a wine tasting at a vineyard near Napier, where the host asked her, 'Would you like to try some Chardonnay?'

She replied, 'My name's not Chardonnay, it's Chantelle!'

Later at the same event she was asked what she thought of a Cloudy Bay and she declared, 'It smells of wine and tastes of grapes!'

Dickie Bird:

While I was umpiring in the World Cup in Pakistan in 1986/87, one of my colleagues gave Javed Miandad out lbw. And if there was one thing you never did in Pakistan, it was to give Javed Miandad out lbw. It was simply not on. The story goes that when that umpire went to heaven, he was met at the Pearly Gates by Saint Peter, who asked him, 'Have you ever done anything wrong?'

The umpire thought for a moment, then replied, 'Well, I do remember once giving Javed Miandad out in a World Cup match in Pakistan. But that was a long time in the past.'

'No, it wasn't,' said Saint Peter. 'It happened just three minutes ago!'

Henry Blofeld:

The 1963/64 England tour of India was notable for one reason. We drew all five Test matches and it was the dullest possible cricket, but I very nearly played in a Test match. We had drawn the first Test in Bangalore but when we got to Bombay, Ken Barrington had gone home, after breaking an arm in a match in Ahmedabad. About four more of the England team were in a hospital called the Sun and Sand in Bombay, suffering from varying degrees of Delhi belly.

On the night before the match, at the press conference, there were only ten fit men, and David Clark, who had captained Kent and was the tour manager, called me into his room. He said, 'Now look, Blowers, you and I are the last two to have played first-class cricket and as you're twenty years younger than me, the axe has fallen on you. You're probably going to have to play tomorrow. Try and get to bed before midnight.' Which I did!

Sadly, the next day Micky Stewart, the vice-captain, recovered well enough to play, so my Test career was nearly . . . but not quite! But I did say one thing to David Clark, which he's never let me forget. Colin Cowdrey and Peter Parfitt were flying out to make up the numbers but they weren't going to get there in time. I told him, 'Now, David, there is one thing. If I get fifty or upwards in either innings, I'm damned if I'm standing down for the Third Test in Calcutta!'

Marcus Berkmann: Rain Men

The most disastrous excursion ever undertaken by the Captain Scott XI combined the dynamics of a cricket tour (male bonding, alcohol, cheap hotels, desultory sightseeing) with the duration and cost of a real holiday (two weeks, and don't ask). The plan was simple – a week in Hong Kong, a week in Delhi, two games in each.

By the time we returned, thirteen days later, virtually no one was talking to anyone else. Small groupings of people who now loathed each other tactfully avoided saying goodbye while they grabbed their luggage and fled to waiting cabs. At Delhi Airport earlier, at least one punch had been thrown. I myself could barely bring myself to spit the names of at least five returning personnel, while my girlfriend, who had also come on the trip, wanted to murder at least eight. Six days later, she gave me the elbow. I developed amoebic dysentery. Credit-card companies wrote pointed letters. It was quite a trip.

But for a writer, no experience is ever wasted. It is with this in mind that I have devised the Cricket Tour Game, which can be played by anyone venturing abroad for spurious cricketing reasons. Score points as instructed, and add up your total. Depending on your point of view, anyone scoring over 200 has done either very well or very badly indeed.

Part 1: At the Airport

You have met at the airport with all your cricketing chums. Score 1 point for any player not there on time. Score 3 points for any player subsequently found hiding in the bar. Score 5 points for every passport that has to be retrieved from a piece of luggage which has already been checked in. Score 10 points for every piece of cricket equipment that goes missing in the process.

PART 2: ON THE AEROPLANE

Long haul, short haul, it doesn't matter. As far as the cricket tourists are concerned, it's time for a drink. Score 4 points for every drink consumed before pubs in England would normally open. Score 5 points for any player who asks for a chaser. Score 1 point for any player who snores loudly during the film. Score 1 point for any player who tries to chat up the stewardess. Score 1 point for each filled barf bag.

PART 3: AT YOUR DESTINATION

Score 2 points for each lost passport, piece of luggage, item of clothing left on plane, etc. Score 5 points for each argument with a passport official ('Can't you read? I am a British subject.') Score 5 points each time you pass the same landmark in the taxi on the way to the hotel. Score 10 points for each argument with the cab driver. Score 3 points if you have hot water in your room. Score 3 points if you have a window.

PART 4: AT THE MATCH

Score 5 points for each humorous 'local rule' dreamed up by the opposition to hamper your efforts. Score 2 points for every terrible lbw decision. If on the Indian subcontinent, score 10 points for every serious stomach ailment contracted from lunch. Score 1 point for every foreign passerby who stops to look at you as though you are mad. Score 1 point for every 36-shot film of useless 'action photos' you take. Score 5 points for any player who forgets his cap and contracts mild sunstroke.

Part 5: Sightseeing

Score 10 points for every player who claims to be fluent in the local language. Score 200 points for every player who really is fluent in the local language. Score 1 point for each unnecessary item you buy, plus an extra point if you have been gratuitously ripped off for it. Score 15 points for each unnecessary item you later manage to palm off on an unsuspecting friend or relative.

Part 6: Late-night Entertainment

Score 25 points for any player (without wife or girlfriend present) who says that he fancies an early night tonight, if that's all right by everyone, and he'll see them all at breakfast. Score 5 points for any player who manages to get through the evening without buying a drink. (Score an extra 50 if that player is you, but only if no one notices.) Score 5 points for anyone who pompously pronounces on the intrinsic superiority of the local beer. Score 2 points for any player who decides to try a local liqueur, 2 more if he pretends to like it, 20 points if he actually likes it. Score 1 point for any player telling any other player at three in the morning, 'You know, Cliff, you're a f***ing good bloke, you really are.'

PART 7: BLOW-UP
Score 1 point for every punch thrown. Score 1 point for every swear word. Score 50 points if you manage to keep out of it completely.

PART 8: THE JOURNEY HOME
Score 5 points per argument, plus an extra 5 if it is with the cab driver again and an extra 10 if the police have to be called. Score 1 point for every player drunk before he gets on the plane. Score 5 points for every player 'accidentally' tripped up in the aisle on his way to the loo. Score 2 points for every player who said he definitely ordered the vegetarian meal, even though you know he didn't. Score 1 point for everyone who says we saw this film on the trip out. Score 1 point for each lost passport, piece of luggage, etc. at the airport. Score 50 points if you speak to any of them ever again.

Andrew Strauss:

Matthew Hoggard doesn't particularly enjoy the limelight. He would rather be out walking his dogs on the Yorkshire Moors than posing on the red carpet at a movie premiere. But behind the slightly dopey 'Farmer Giles' exterior is a surprisingly sharp mind. He does not like people knowing it but he has three high-grade A levels to his name. I am not sure if it would ruin his credibility up on the Yorkshire Moors if he admitted to being clever, but in his intellect, rather like his bowling, he prefers to be underestimated.

Communicating with him before 10 a.m. is a nightmare, and even the most good-natured of comments are likely to be greeted with a Neanderthal grunt. He is blunt and to the point with anyone who cares to listen. An example of this came on England's 2005/06 winter tour of India.

In Delhi the England team were invited to the British High Commission for a huge party to celebrate the Queen's eightieth birthday. Prince Charles and Camilla were at the do and, as Camilla came through the room on her own, Hoggard caught her eye. He said, in the same way he would engage a team-mate, 'Don't tell me that you're sneaking out of here before the party's over. If you are, though, I'm coming with you!'

Dickie Bird:

One of the problems, in both India and Pakistan, is that spectators are a fruity lot, inclined to hurl all manner of it at players unfortunate enough to be stationed on the boundary edge. During a Test match in Pakistan in 1969, the New Zealand opener Bruce Murray, known as 'Bags' because of his initials (B.A.G. Murray), was down on the third-man boundary, and he must have felt as though his head was the target on a coconut shy.

Finally, he could stand it no longer and complained to his captain, Graham Dowling, who threatened to stop the game if anything else was thrown at Murray. Not long afterwards, an expertly aimed banana, travelling at a fair old lick, flew over the fence and became, quite literally, a pain in the neck for poor old Bags.

He bent down, picked up the missile and ran towards the middle, brandishing it in the air. At the same time, the bowler, Dayle Hadlee – brother of Richard – set off on his run, quite oblivious of what was happening, and he failed to hear Dowling's shout to abort the delivery. He let Asif Iqbal have a short riser, which was fended into the vacant gully area. Or, at least, it was vacant before Bags arrived just in time to take a peach of a diving catch, coming up with the ball in one hand and the banana in the other.

He must have felt a bit of a lemon when the umpire called dead ball!

EXTRAS

Mike Selvey:

It is a gloriously sunny day in early June and the crowds are already milling along the St John's Wood Road, chattering animatedly as they make their way towards the Grace Gates. It is Test match day at Lord's. A white Jaguar noses noiselessly past cabs dropping members off, and pulls up at the gates. The occupant, blond, six feet eight inches tall, and pretty recognisable in these parts, waits patiently for the gates to swing open and admit him. He waits in vain until at last they open a crack and an elderly gent walks out and peers myopically into the car. The driver pushes a button and the window hisses down. 'Can I see your pass, sir?' asks the old man.

The only thing that Tony Greig could do was laugh. He might as well have done; everyone else did. 'Sorry, I haven't got one,' he replied.

'Well, you can't come in here, then,' the England captain was told, and the man shambled back inside and closed the gates once more.

If the England captain couldn't get into the head-quarters of cricket, what hope is there for the rest of us? The short answer is none. Once, when I played for Middlesex, I was refused entry to the ground on the morning of a big match, a cup semi-final maybe, by someone with whom I had passed pleasantries on probably half the summers' mornings for the previous ten years.

On another occasion, a policeman actually reached in through my car window during an inquisition at the gate and confiscated my keys to prevent me getting further. And once I was not allowed into the pavilion 'because Middlesex aren't at home today'. I would not have minded so much if it had been a Test or something, but it was 4 January, the snow lay thick on the ground, and I had only called in while passing to wish people a Happy New Year!

Barry Johnston:

The former Prime Minister Sir John Major had to give up playing cricket in the 1960s after he injured his leg in a very serious car crash in Nigeria. Many years later he was introduced to a woman who claimed to have mystical powers. Recalling the incident, John Major says that the woman told him, very apologetically, that his car accident had been a mistake. She explained, 'It should have happened to the car in front.'

Major was not quite sure how to respond to that, so he asked her, 'Can fate put my leg back together again?'

'Much too difficult,' said the mystic. 'Leg broken, ligaments torn, kneecap smashed, not a hope of putting it together again. But I can probably give you a wish as a consolation prize.'

'Excellent,' said Major. 'Please spare us an England middle order collapse in the next Test match.'

The mystic paused and said, 'Let me have another look at that leg!'

Ian Wooldridge:

In the summer of 1976 I was watching a cricket match at The Oval in London. There was an intriguing advertisement along the boundary fence to the left of the Vauxhall End sightscreen. In large letters it bore the words MikroPul Ducon. In smaller letters it said Environmental Protection.

The only problem about MikroPul Ducon, as advertised at The Oval and therefore on BBC television, was whether you purchased it by the quart, the yard, the kilo or in packets of three.

'No doubt about it,' said my informant. 'It's the most brilliant coup of the year. It's a Greek firm, you know. Trust the Greeks to think up that "environmental protection" line.'

The implications, of course, were huge. If the BBC had banned Grand Prix motor racing from their screens because some of the cars roar around with Durex written all over them, how could they conceivably televise the Fifth Test from The Oval with MikroPul Ducon staring you in the face every time the ball ran down to the Vauxhall Stand boundary?

Well, millions of bewildered televiewers *had* seen it on Wednesday when the BBC screened the one-day Surrey–Essex match. So, bristling with puritanical outrage, one felt it only right to telephone the Surrey Cricket Club and castigate them for the offensive tastelessness of their boundary advertising.

'Oh my God,' said a Surrey spokesman. 'Is *that* what they are? It never occurred to us. I say, you're not going to print this, are you? You realise that the Fifth Test will be blacked out on television?'

'It is the duty of a free press to protect young children and elderly ladies from being affronted by this kind of nauseating advertising,' we boomed. 'Motor racing? Cricket? What's the difference?'

A low moan from The Oval indicated they knew all was lost.

To conclude our inquiries we called at a chemist's in London, EC4, waited until two lady typists had bought some shampoo, gestured a male assistant to the end of the counter and whispered: 'Three MikroPul Ducons, please.'

'I'm afraid I've never heard of the products, sir,' said the assistant.

'Really,' we replied nastily, 'of course, they *are* the very latest and presumably only very *up-to-date* stores stock them for really *discerning* clients.'

'Possibly, sir,' said the assistant.

So the search widened.

'Awfully sorry,' said a worthy-sounding man at the Family Planning Association, 'we don't seem to have them on our recommended list.'

'What on earth,' demanded a businesslike lady at the Association of the British Pharmaceutical Industry, 'are you talking about?'

'Very sorry old boy,' said a jolly chap at the Ann Summers establishment up near Marble Arch, 'can't help you out at all.'

'If they're rivals of ours,' said a big wheel at the London Rubber Company somewhat brusquely, 'we've never heard of them.'

'I've just searched through all our reference books,' said an infinitely helpful secretary on the *Chemist and Druggist Directory*, 'and they don't appear to be here. A Greek firm, you say?'

'Yes, a Greek firm,' we replied testily and promptly rang our correspondent in Athens to track down, once and for all, these Hellenic environmental protectionists whose cunning advertising was about to wipe cricket off English television screens.

He drew a blank.

It was fast approaching teatime on the cricket grounds of England when we received a telephone call from a man in Shoeburyness, Essex.

'I understand from Surrey Cricket Club,' he said pleasantly, 'that you wish to buy an air-conditioning unit?'

'Are you some kind of nutcase?' we demanded. 'Get off the line.'

'No,' he replied, 'I am the managing director of MikroPul Ducon, manufacturers of filters for cleaning dirty industrial and domestic air.'

'Do you sell anything in packets of three which have to be sent out under plain cover?' we asked weakly.

'Certainly not,' he retorted, 'air filters is our business and we are cricket fans to a man.'

'Thank you for calling,' we said. 'Forgive us our trespassing.'

'Not at all,' said Mr MikroPul Ducon. 'I'll send you a price list.'

Barry Johnston:

On the Australian tour of the West Indies in 1984, their flamboyant batsman Dean Jones wandered on to the beach one day and saw his team-mates having fielding practice, but in a most unusual way – they were standing neck deep in the sea, throwing the ball to one another. The Australian team has always come up with innovative methods of practice and Jones was an enthusiastic fielder, so he decided to join in. Ever the showman, Dean Jones didn't simply walk into the sea, he broke into a sprint along the beach and performed a spectacular dive into the waves – only to land face down on the sand covered by about a foot of water.

His team-mates burst out laughing. They had set him up by kneeling in the sea to make it look like the water level was higher than it was. Not surprisingly, Jones ended up with a very sore neck. His recovery was not helped by his team-mates frequently calling out, 'Hey Deano!' and getting the giggles every time he turned towards them, causing further painful twinges to his already stiff neck.

Simon Hughes:

One day I was twelfth man at Lord's and I was having a breather on the balcony after the morning chores, watching Wilf Slack bat. Suddenly he larruped one straight into the Northants short-leg's head. The fielder sank to the ground in agony and all the Middlesex players looked at me as if it were my fault. 'Go on, hurry up, get the physio – he might be dying,' said the coach.

The Middlesex physiotherapist was Johnny Miller, a frail elderly man, who was almost blind. Miller was in his room and when I burst in, he sensed something was wrong.

'What is it, mate?' he asked. 'An MCC member with convulsions?'

'No, something serious – Geoff Cook's been hit on the head.'

'Quick, lead me out,' he said, panicking, and grabbed his first-aid satchel, knocking bottles off the medicine cabinet in the process.

I helped him downstairs and through the Long Room, but when we were out on the field he let go of my hand and suddenly blundered ahead. He lurched towards a group of players crowded round the stricken Cook, then suddenly veered off course and made straight for the wicket-keeper, George Sharp, who was minding his own business by the stumps.

'Where's the problem, mate?' Miller asked, and started feeling Sharp's face. 'Oh yes, a nasty bump there.'

'That's my gumshield,' said Sharp. 'The injured player's over there!'

Barry Johnston:

It was the first day of a recent Test match between England and Australia at Lord's. A smartly dressed, athletic figure strode up to the Grace Gates to collect his ticket, which had been left for him by one of the England players. He approached one of the famous Lord's gatemen.

'Excuse me, has a ticket for Lord Coe been left here by one of the players?'

'I'll have a look, sir, but I don't remember any name like that. No, I am afraid there isn't one here.'

'Are you sure? It's for Lord Coe, the chairman of the London 2012 Organising Committee.'

'No, I'm sorry, sir. But sometimes tickets are left at the North Gate on the other side of the ground.'

'No, he definitely said the Grace Gates. Surely you recognise me? I'm Sebastian Coe, the double Olympic gold medallist and world record breaker in the 800 metres, 1,500 metres and the mile.'

'Well, I wouldn't know about that, sir, but if you really are Sebastian Coe, it shouldn't take you too long to run round to the North Gate!'

Brian Johnston:

I heard this story from the veteran comedy actor Naunton Wayne, who starred in the Alfred Hitchcock film *The Lady Vanishes,* and was a great cricket fan. Before the start of a needle village match, the home captain found he was one short. In desperation he was looking round the ground for someone he could rope in to play when he spotted an old horse grazing quietly in the field next door. So he went up to him and asked him if he would like to make up the side. The horse stopped eating and said, 'Well, I haven't played for some time and am a bit out of practice but if you're pushed, I'll certainly help you out,' and so saying jumped over the fence and sat down in a deck-chair in front of the pavilion.

The visitors lost the toss and the home side batted first, the horse being put in last. They were soon 23 for 9 and the horse made his way to the wicket wearing those sort of leather shoes horses have on when they are pulling a roller or a mower. He soon showed his eye was well in and hit the bowling all over the field. When he wasn't hitting sixes he was galloping for quick singles and never once said 'Neigh' when his partner called him for a run. Finally he was out hoof before wicket for a brilliant 68, and the home side had made 99.

When the visitors batted, the home captain put the horse in the deep and he saved many runs by galloping round the boundary and hoofing the ball back to the wicket-keeper. However, the visitors were not losing any wickets and were soon 50 for 0. The home captain had tried all his regular bowlers in vain when he suddenly thought of the horse. He had batted brilliantly and now was fielding better than anyone. At least he could do no worse than the other bowlers. So he called out to him, 'Horse, would you like to take the next over at the vicarage end?'

The horse looked surprised, 'Of course I wouldn't,' he replied. 'Whoever heard of a horse who could *bowl*!'

Michael Simkins: Fatty Batter

One of the wonderful things about cricket is the way it throws up unlikely heroes. The Harry Baldwin Occasionals XI away against Worthing Railways is just such an occasion.

The venue is Patcham Place and the match is supposed to begin at 2 p.m., but by 3.15 it has yet to commence. Of the eleven players who should have turned up for the Baldwins, so far we have three. A glance at the main road skirting the ground is all that's needed to see what the problem is. Patcham Place runs directly alongside the main A23 London to Brighton road, and today's match has coincided with the annual London to Brighton cycle rally, in aid of the British Heart Foundation. There are between 25,000 and 30,000 cyclists all approaching the town centre along a twenty-mile stretch of the A23, behind which founders a vehicle traffic jam that is already stretching back nearly fifteen miles. Somewhere in the middle of that lot, cooking quietly on a low heat, is the cream of today's Baldwin team.

Which leaves myself, Keith the Cub Scout leader, whom I rang twenty minutes ago to whisk away from his youngest's birthday party, and finally our impromptu substitute, Gordon Quill.

Quill is one of the curios of the side. He readily admits to being hopeless at the game but likes to come along to watch and afterwards enjoy a blackcurrant and lemonade in the pub with us all. He doesn't really play much, but deals in antique Victoriana, and he's only come along to today's match in order to show me his collection of antique seaside postcards he picked up at an auction in Lewes last week.

The Worthing Railways captain comes up to me. A large bluff man called Frank, he works as a ticket inspector on the Three Bridges to Arundel spur.

'How many are you now?'

'Um . . .'

'Never mind. Let's go.'

'Of course, of course. It's just that . . .'

'What?'

'Well, it's just that we forgot it was the bike rally today . . .'

'Tough.' In his professional life Frank is used to lame excuses and pleas of ignorance. 'We'll lend you a couple of fielders till they arrive.'

He pulls on his batting gloves and summons his opening partner to join him in the middle. I call across to Quill who is just showing a first-edition postcard of Donald McGill's 'I Can't Find My Little Willy' to the Worthing Railways wicket-keeper.

'Gordon, you're going to have to open the bowling.'

Having Gordon Quill open the bowling is a bit like asking my mum to front a twelve-part television cookery course. But the fact is there's nobody else. At least Quill can just about propel it down the other end. We'll get through his first over and then regroup. Perhaps somebody else might have turned up by then.

The Railwaymen have lent us three of their team, all of whom are standing sulkily in the outfield waiting to be positioned. I hand Quill the match ball provided by the opposition, a gleaming rock-hard cherry still in its tissue paper, and retire to mid-off to consider my tactical options.

There's no delaying the inevitable. Quill approaches off a run-up of about three inches, and whirls his arm over. The ball bounces three times before coming to rest just in front of Frank's motionless figure at the crease. Frank removes his helmet and stares over at me with a look of withering disdain.

'Is he taking the piss?'

'Not at all.'

'This is your opening bowler is it?'

I scan the roadside before replying. Just an endless crawl of slowly moving traffic. 'Just at the moment,' I reply.

'Right,' mutters Frank, simply. He picks up the ball and throws it back to Quill. 'Here you are, Dr Livingstone,' he says. Quill marches back to his run-up and sets off again.

Three seconds later, via a brief but violent interruption in its trajectory from Frank's bat, the ball soars over my head at extra cover, hits a tree on the boundary halfway up its trunk, ricochets into the road where it nearly decapitates a member of the Crawley Down Road Racing team, before bouncing off the far pavement and coming to rest against the wall of the Black Lion Hotel. Keith trots off to fetch it, but with the cyclists still surging past in an endless flood, the simple act of crossing and recrossing the road eats up a further five minutes.

The next ball is hit with such force that it breaks a security light outside the front door of the YMCA hostel at the far end of the ground. Quill looks nervously over at me, but I give him a thumbs-up sign to indicate he's doing just fine. Frank thrashes his next delivery as hard as he can straight back at the bowler, but fortunately it narrowly misses Quill and cannons into the far set of stumps beside him, not only preventing any runs from being scored but breaking one of the bails in the process. Further minutes tick by while some binding tape is found from the pavilion and the wicket is repaired.

Quill's fifth delivery is flayed over extra cover, where it strikes the hub cap of a Peugeot 406 travelling on the main road, and rebounds back on to the field of play. My heart momentarily leaps: perhaps the driver will pull over, using up yet more time. But he drives on, oblivious. Funny how when luck's against you . . .

But at last fortune turns my way. Quill's last delivery is smashed for six high over the midwicket boundary, where it lands deep into a huge bank of nettles and fallen tree trunks brought down by the great storm of 1985.

After furious exhortations from Frank to the pavilion, his grumbling colleagues eventually rise from their deckchairs and begin a slow and painstaking search for the missing ball. Quill turns to me ruefully. 'Sorry old chap,' he says.

But there's no need for an apology. He's playing a blinder. Success on the field is all about percentage cricket, and with the current wage restraint being imposed on British Rail platform staff combined with a brand new cricket ball retailing at nearly fifteen quid a pop, there's no way this lot are going to give up the hunt for it easily. By the time the precious ball is found lying behind a rotting tree stump, the clock on the YMCA building is showing nearly 4 o'clock.

The Railwaymen celebrate the discovery with a yell of triumph, but even as the ball is being thrown back on to the pitch, I spot our first-change bowler Rex Scudamore's Volvo pulling into the car park at the far end. What's more he's already changed into his whites and is ready to play. Phil Coleridge's Renault is only thirty yards behind. I celebrate by giving my emergency bowler a huge hug of gratitude. The hits into the cyclists, the broken bail, and the disappearance among the nettles: Quill's single over may have conceded thirty runs, but crucially it has occupied nearly half an hour. He's got us through our crisis. Mafeking has been relieved. Game on.

MATCH REPORT:

Harry Baldwins vs Worthing Railways
Worthing Railways 103 all out off 18 overs
(Quill 0-30, Scudamore 5-22)
Baldwins 104-4
Harry Baldwins win by 6 wickets

Fred Trueman:

The terminology of cricket has changed over the years. Many of the terms I knew now seem to have a totally different meaning. Here are what some common cricketing terms appear to mean now:

Fielding restrictions The laws that make a captain place fielders in positions where he doesn't want them.

Twenty20 Ironically, lack of vision on the part of the game's administrators.

Leg-break bowler Twelfth man.

Maiden over Unattainable quest in Twenty20.

Full toss Journeyman bowler's attempt at a yorker.

Spearhead bowling attack Three or four bowlers hell bent on defending.

Day/nighter One-day game, the starting time of which has been changed from when most people are at work in the morning to when most people are at work in the afternoon.

All-rounder Player who is average at more things than the average player.

Central contract Piece of paper that ensures a player is a county player in name only.

Opening batsman Most likely winner of Man of the Match award.

World Cup final Australia versus somebody else.

Required run rate A figure per over which the upper-order batsmen have set their lower-order batsmen in order to gain victory.

Slower ball This used to be a delivery bowled at a much-reduced pace than previous deliveries and bowled at the end of an over to surprise a batsman. Now the norm.

Spinner Slow medium-pacer with short run-up.

NatWest Trophy Gone West Trophy.

Genuine fast bowler Medium-fast.

High-fives Opportunity when wicket is taken for third man to get himself on TV.

One of the game's true characters Wears an earring.

Loyal county player Never been approached by another county.

Reduced target A modernism of cricket whereby statistical superiority can be achieved through practical inferiority.

Has been offered the light But will never see it.

County membership Whereby supporters fork out £300 a season to see their team perform devoid of its best players.

'AGGERS, DO STOP IT!'

Barry Johnston:

Before the start of the regular *Test Match Special* broadcast in the summer of 1993 there was an extra half-hour programme at 10.30 a.m. on Radio Five, presented by Jonathan Agnew. It began with an upbeat signature tune which required Jonathan to give a summary of the state of play in exactly seven seconds, sounding more like a Radio One disc-jockey than a Radio Three cricket commentator. He used to practise it over and over in order to get the timing right and Brian Johnston always found it most amusing.

On the Sunday morning of the Test match at Headingley, Brian was the first one in the commentary box as usual, when Peter Baxter, the *Test Match Special* producer, rushed in to say that Agnew was going to be late and he would have to do the Radio Five programme instead. With only minutes to spare, Brian had to write and rehearse his seven-second summary, speaking ever faster over the signature tune, as Baxter kept urging him to do it one more time. 'Still a bit long, Johnners . . .

need to lose another second if you can . . .' After several, increasingly frantic, attempts it was time to go on air and, being the consummate professional, Brian did it perfectly.

It was only then that Agnew burst laughing into the box and Brian realised that he had been had. There *was* no Radio Five programme on Sunday morning. The engineers had recorded the whole episode and for the rest of the day Agnew gleefully played the tape to anyone who would listen, saying that Brian had been unable to get the summary right. 'In fact he was spot on first time,' recalls Baxter, 'as I knew he would be.'

'It made up into a brilliant tape,' says Richie Benaud. 'It was funny and a very good practical joke which Brian took in good part. Trouble was, Aggers wanted to tell the world about it. I thought at the time that this could be a very dangerous thing to do.'

Brian did not wait long to exact his revenge. 'He worked on the basis of never get angry, just get even,' adds Benaud, 'and when he played a joke it was always a beauty. The one he came up with during the next Test at Edgbaston was a ripper. It remains my favourite.'

On the Saturday morning of the match Keith Mackenzie, the producer/director of BBC TV cricket, approached Agnew and asked him if he would record an interview for *Grandstand* during the lunch interval. The subject was to be England's lack of fast bowlers.

The interview had to be precisely ten minutes long and hard-hitting in content. Mackenzie also dropped a hint that there might at some stage be a place for someone new in the television team.

Agnew readily agreed and that lunchtime he sat in front of the cameras with Fred Trueman and Jack Bannister, both former fast bowlers and now respected cricket experts, to record the interview. Trueman was puffing on a huge cigar which he blew over Agnew just before they began. Undeterred, Agnew put his first question to Bannister, who replied bluntly, 'I've got no idea.' He turned quickly to Trueman, who took another long puff on his cigar and muttered darkly, 'Don't know.'

Agnew began to sweat, not helped by Keith Mackenzie yelling in his earpiece that it was the worst interview he had ever seen. The minutes ticked slowly by. Trueman, when asked about pitches, wandered off into a dissertation on fly-fishing and its benefits to fast bowlers in the strengthening of the shoulder muscles. Bannister contributed an unrelated story about the wrist spinner Eric Hollies and how he almost won a game against Lindsay Hassett's Australian side in 1953. The final straw was when Trueman began talking about damp-proof courses.

At the end of the longest ten minutes of his life, Agnew handed back to the mythical *Grandstand* studio in despair, saying, 'I don't think we have answered too many questions there, gentlemen.' He sat stunned in his chair, imagining his television career to be in ruins. Suddenly his earpiece crackled into life. 'I think the veteran long-nosed commentator might have got his revenge!' chuckled a well-known voice. Brian had been sitting alongside Keith Mackenzie throughout the interview.

He had persuaded the whole of the BBC TV outside broadcast team to give up their lunch break, simply to set up Agnew. You did not beat the Master that easily!

Brian Johnston:

I've said that cricket is fun. Now I want you to cast your mind back to August 1991, the Friday of The Oval Test match against the West Indies. Bad light stopped play at half past six and Peter Baxter, our producer, turned to Jonathan Agnew and myself and said, 'Go through the scorecard, will you please, to fill in time.'

Gallantly, I started the scorecard. I got down as far as Ian Botham, who had been out 'hit wicket' and this is what followed:

Johnners: Botham, in the end, out in the most extra-ordinary way.

Aggers: Oh, it was ever so sad really. It was interesting, because we were talking and he had just started to loosen up. He had started to look, perhaps, for the big blows through the off side, for anything a little bit wide – and I remember saying, 'It looks as if Ian Botham is just starting to play his old way.'

It was a bouncer and he tried to hook it. Why he tried to hook Ambrose, I'm not sure, because on this sort of pitch it's a very difficult prospect. It smacked him on the helmet, I think – I'm not quite sure where it did actually hit him . . .'

Johnners: Shoulder, I think.

Aggers: Shoulder, was it? As he tried to hook, he lost his balance, and he knew – this is the tragic thing about it – he knew exactly what was going to happen. He tried to step over the stumps and just flicked a bail with his right pad.

Johnners: He more or less tried to do the splits over it and, unfortunately, the inner part of his thigh must have just removed the bail.

Aggers: He just didn't quite get his leg over!

Johnners: Anyhow (*chuckles*) . . . (*clatter as Bill Frindall drops his stopwatch in surprise*) . . . he did very well indeed, batting one hundred and thirty-one minutes and hit three fours . . . (*Agnew buries his face in his hands and starts to giggle helplessly*) . . . and then we had Lewis playing extremely well for forty-seven not out . . . Aggers, do stop it . . . (*Frindall laughs in background*) . . . and he was joined by DeFreitas who was in for forty minutes, a useful little partnership there. They put on thirty-five in forty minutes and then he was caught by Dujon off Walsh . . . (*snort from Frindall*). Lawrence, always entertaining, batted for thirty-five . . . (*Johnners starts to wheeze*) . . . thirty-five . . . (*gasping*) . . . minutes . . . hit a four over the wicket-keeper's h . . . (*high-pitched giggle*) . . . Aggers, for goodness sake stop it . . . he hit a f . . . (*dissolves into uncontrollable laughter. Peter Baxter hisses at Agnew to say something.*)

Aggers: Yes, Lawrence . . . extremely well . . . (*collapses completely*).

Both men are now speechless with laughter, tears rolling down their faces. Agnew turns desperately for help to Tony Cozier, sitting at the microphone on his left, busily writing an article on his word-processor. Cozier – a frequent victim of Brian's practical jokes – looks up and winks at Agnew, grins and carries on with his typing. Brian tries gamely to continue with the scorecard.

Johnners: (*Hysterical*) . . . He hit . . . (*his voice getting higher and higher*) he hit a four over the wicket-keeper's head and he was out for nine . . . (*crying and dabbing at his eyes with a large handkerchief*) . . . and Tufnell came in and batted for twelve minutes, then he was caught by Haynes off Patterson for two . . . (*calming down gradually*) . . . and there were fifty-four extras and England were all out for four hundred and nineteen . . . I've stopped laughing now . . .

Barry Johnston:

Next morning the letters and phone calls started to flood in to the *Test Match Special* commentary box. Thousands of drivers had been listening in their cars on their way home and many of them had been forced to pull into the side of the road until they had calmed down. Tim Rice laughed so hard that he thought he was going to endanger his fellow motorists. Ronnie Corbett rang to say that his wife Ann had to stop on the hard shoulder of the M1.

A listener called Paul Brookbanks wrote that he was laughing out loud when he pulled up behind a police car at some road-works in Peterborough. The policeman got out of his car and walked slowly back to the driver to ask him exactly what he found so amusing – just as Brian returned to normal. The poor man tried to explain that he had been listening to a cricket commentary on the radio, but he could tell that the policeman did not believe a word of it.

Another listener, Jane Wardman from Leeds, had been confined to bed for several weeks with pneumonia. She was feeling fed-up and depressed. Then she heard the 'leg-over' incident on the radio and for the first time in many weeks, wrote Jane, 'laughed until the tears streamed down my face'.

There were even reports of a two-mile tail-back at the

entrance to the Dartford Tunnel on the M25, because some drivers were laughing so much that they were unable to go through the toll-booths.

On the Monday following the broadcast the BBC's Head of Litigation, Diana Adie, received an urgent fax from Tony Alexander, a solicitor with a firm called Heffrons in Milton Keynes. It read as follows:

Dear Sir,

Re: Cricket Commentary – Friday, 9 August 1991.

We have been consulted by Mr Wally Painter and his wife Dolly. On Friday evening our clients were in the process of redecorating their hallway. Mr Painter was perched on a ladder in the stairwell of his house, whilst Mrs Painter held the ladder steady. Our clients' aquarium with assorted tropical fish was situated at the foot of the stairwell.

Our clients are keen cricket enthusiasts, and were listening to the summary of the day's play on Radio Three, when Mr Brian Johnston and Mr Jon Agnew were discussing Mr Ian Botham's dismissal, which apparently involved some footwork which Mr Botham failed to consummate.

The ensuing events caused a vibration in the ladder and, in spite of Mrs Painter's firm grasp, Mr Painter fell off the ladder, landing awkwardly on the partial landing, thereby dislocating his left wrist. The ladder fell on Mrs Painter, who suffered a contusion to her forehead.

The 5 litre drum of Dulux Sandalwood Emulsion fell and crashed through the aquarium, which flooded the hallway, depositing various frantically flapping exotic fish onto a Persian rug. The Painters' pedigree Persian cat (Mr Painter spent many years in Tehran as an adviser to the late Shah) grabbed one of the fish, a Malayan red-spined Gurnot, and promptly choked to death.

The water seeped down into the cellar where the electricity meters are located. There were several short circuits, which resulted in (a) the main switchboard being severely damaged and (b) the burglar alarm (which is connected to the local police station) being set off.

Meanwhile, Mr and Mrs Painter were staggering towards the bathroom, apparently in paroxysms of hysterical laughter despite their injuries. Within minutes, the police arrived, and believing the Painters to be vandals and suspecting, as both were incoherent, that they had been taking drugs, promptly arrested them.

We are now instructed to inform you that our clients hold the Corporation liable for:-

(a) *Their personal injuries.*

(b) *The loss of the aquarium and various exotic fish collected over several years.*

(c) *The damage to the Persian rug.*

(d) *Damage to the electrical installation and burglar alarm.*

(e) *Death of the cat.*

However, they are prepared to settle all claims for damages in respect of the above provided that you supply them with a recording of the discussion between Mr Johnston and Mr Agnew, together with an undertaking from Mr Johnston and Mr Agnew that they will not in future discuss Mr Botham's footwork or lack of it, while Mr and Mrs Painter are decorating their property.

Yours faithfully,
Heffrons.

I am happy to report that the Painters received their tape.

ACKNOWLEDGEMENTS

I would like to express my grateful thanks to all the authors and publishers who have given their permission for extracts from their work to be reproduced in this book. I would also like to thank Tony Alexander for the use of his letter about the Ian Botham 'leg over' incident. My special thanks to John Ireland for his brilliant illustrations. I am also most grateful to Rupert Lancaster and Roddy Bloomfield at Hodder & Stoughton for their invaluable advice and to my copy-editor, Marion Paull, for her excellent work correcting the manuscript.

Extracts from the following books and CDs have been reproduced by kind permission of their publishers:

Atherton, Michael: *Opening Up* (Hodder & Stoughton, 2003); Bell, Angus: *Batting on the Bosphorus: A Skoda-powered Cricket Tour Through Eastern Europe* (Canongate Books Ltd, Edinburgh, 2008); Benaud, Richie: *My Spin on Cricket* (Hodder & Stoughton, 2005); Berkmann, Marcus: *Rain Men* (Little, Brown Book Group, 1995); Bird, Dickie: *An Evening with Dickie Bird* (Hodder Headline Audiobooks, 1998); Bird, Dickie: *White Cap and Bails* (Hodder & Stoughton,

1999); Blofeld, Henry: *An Evening with Blowers* (Hodder Headline Audiobooks, 2002); Blofeld, Henry: *Cricket's Great Entertainers* (Hodder & Stoughton, 2003); Brayshaw, Ian: *The Wit of Cricket* (The Currawong Press, Sydney, Australia, 1981); England, Chris: *Balham to Bollywood* (Hodder & Stoughton, 2002); Flintoff, Andrew: *Being Freddie* (Hodder & Stoughton, 2005); Fowler, Graeme: *Fox on the Run* (Viking, Penguin Books Ltd, 1988); Frindall, Bill: *Bearders: My Life in Cricket* (Orion Non-Fiction, a division of The Orion Publishing Group, 2006); Gough, Darren: *Dazzler: The Autobiography* (Michael Joseph, Penguin Books Ltd, 2001); Heald, Tim: *My Lord's* (HarperCollins Publisher, 1990); Hughes, Simon: *A Lot of Hard Yakka* (Headline, 1997); Johnson, Martin: *Can't Bat, Can't Bowl, Can't Field* (HarperCollins Publisher, 1997); Johnston, Barry: *Johnners: The Life of Brian* (Hodder & Stoughton, 2003); Johnston, Brian & Johnston, Barry: *An Evening with Johnners* (Partridge Press, 1996); Johnston, Brian: *An Evening with Johnners* (Hodder Headline Audiobooks, 2000); Johnston, Brian: *The Wit of Cricket* (Leslie Frewin, 1968); Lloyd, David: *The Autobiography* (HarperCollins Publisher, 2000); Parkinson, Michael: *On Cricket* (Hodder & Stoughton, 2003); Pietersen, Kevin: *Crossing the Boundary* (Ebury, The Random House Group Ltd, 2006); Rice, Jonathan: *Classic After-Dinner Sports Tales* (HarperCollins Publisher,

2004); Simkins, Michael: *Fatty Batter* (Ebury, The Random House Group Ltd, 2007); Strauss, Andrew: *Coming into Play* (Hodder & Stoughton, 2006); Thompson, Harry: *Penguins Stopped Play* (John Murray, 2006); Trueman, Fred: *As It Was* (Pan Macmillan, London, 2004); Trueman, Fred & Mosey, Don: *Talking Cricket* (Hodder & Stoughton, 1997); Vaughan, Michael: *A Year in the Sun* (Hodder & Stoughton, 2003); Warne, Shane: *My Autobiography* (Hodder & Stoughton, 2001); Wooldridge, Ian: *Searching for Heroes* (Hodder & Stoughton, 2007); Bird, Dickie; Blofeld, Henry; Johnston, Brian: *The Wit of Cricket* (Hodder Headline Audiobooks, 2004); Benaud, Richie; Bird, Dickie; Blofeld, Henry; Johnston, Brian; Trueman, Fred: *The Wit of Cricket 2* (Hodder & Stoughton Audiobooks, 2007).

Amongst other books and websites consulted, particular use was made of: Christopher Martin-Jenkins: *The Complete Who's Who of Test Cricketers*; *Wisden Cricketers' Almanack*; *Daily Mail*; anecdotage. com; bbc.co.uk; cricinfo.com; heraldsun.com.au; indiancricketfans.com; oregoncricket.googlepages.com. Whilst every effort has been made to trace all copyright holders, the publishers would be pleased to hear from any not here acknowledged.

INDEX

Index

Index

Index

THE WIT OF CRICKET

Now available on audio CD, here is a bumper collection of
funny stories and anecdotes form the world of cricket as
told by five of the game's all-time great personalities – Richie
Benaud, Dickie Bird, Henry Blofeld, Brian Johnston and
Fred Trueman.

Recorded live in theatres and in the studio, here are dozens
of hilarious anecdotes about Test cricketers and England
players – as well as some of the most famous gaffes and
practical jokes carried out by the commentary team on
BBC Radio's *Test Match Special*.

Enjoy the best storytellers in the business as they prove
that cricket is a funny game – even when rain stops play!

Available on audio CD from Hodder & Stoughton

www.hodder.co.uk

THE WIT OF GOLF

A bumper bag of humorous anecdotes and amusing tales from golf's best-loved personalities that proves golf is a funny old game – birdies, bunkers and all!

Read hilarious stories covering everything from caddies to the clubhouse by the game's all-time great characters, including Peter Alliss, Nick Faldo, Sandy Lyle, Sam Torrance and Ian Woosnam. Enjoy the humour of legendary players such as Seve Ballesteros, Tony Jacklin, Jack Nicklaus, Lee Trevino and Tiger Woods, as they share the funny side of playing in the Open Championship and the Ryder Cup.

The Wit of Golf is a wonderful collection of jokes, stories and anecdotes, perfect for any golf fan.

Available in hardback and on audio CD
from Hodder & Stoughton

www.hodder.co.uk